18th CENTURY PROPHECY

The time will come, when thou shalt lift thine eyes
To watch a long-drawn battle in the skies,
While aged peasants, too amazed for words,
Stare at the flying fleets of wond'rous birds.
England, so long the mistress of the sea,
Where winds and waves confess her sovereignty,
Her ancient triumphs yet on high shall bear,
And reign, the sovereign of the conquered air.

(Translated from Gray's 'Luna Habitabilis', Cambridge 1737)

Wartime Teesside
revisited

Bill Norman

Bill Norman
2004

Published in 2004 by
Bill Norman, 23a Thames Avenue,
Guisborough, Cleveland, TS14 8AE
England.

ISBN 0-9547325-0-2

Other books by Bill Norman.

Wartime Teesside
Luftwaffe over the North
Failed to Return
No.640(Halifax)Squadron, Leconfield
Broken Eagles (Luftwaffe losses over Yorkshire, 1939-1945)
Broken Eagles 2 (Luftwaffe losses over Northumberland & Durham, 1939-1945)

Introduction

When the Dalesman Publishing Company published my first book, *Wartime Teesside,* in 1989, I had already been researching aspects of the Second World War in the North of England for a number of years. Fifteen years and six books later, my curiosity about wartime events in the northern area is stronger than it ever was.

Prior to 1984, my interest had been spasmodic but my attitude changed decisively in that year, when I appealed to readers of the Middlesbrough *Evening Gazette* for eye-witness accounts of the daylight bombing raid on that town's railway station on Bank Holiday Monday, 3 August, 1942. The response was impressive: written replies totalled almost 100 and there were sufficient telephone calls to keep me occupied for nearly six hours on the night that the appeal appeared in the newspaper.

Many respondents who could provide only part of the story took the opportunity to ask for fuller details of what had happened on that day many years earlier. Others who had more information to offer did not restrict their accounts to the events of 3 August, 1942: they mentioned other incidents too, some of which I was aware; others of which I was not. Curiosity was aroused and my investigation widened. Some of the results of those broader-based researches subsequently appeared in my second book, *Luftwaffe over the North,* which was published by Leo Cooper/Pen & Sword Books in 1993 and reprinted in 1997.

Like the concentric circles formed by a pebble dropping into a mill pond, the public response to my second book widened my interest further and subsequently introduced me to men who had flown with the Royal Air Force in wartime and also led to my meeting ex-Luftwaffe crews who had operated over the northern counties during 1939-45.

Four further books arose from those contacts: *Failed to Return* (Leo Cooper/Pen & Sword, 1995) and *No.640(Halifax)Squadron, Leconfield* (privately published in 1999) dealt with the trials and tribulations of bomber crews operating from Yorkshire airfields; *Broken Eagles (Luftwaffe losses over Yorkshire)* and *Broken Eagles 2(Luftwaffe losses over Northumberland & Durham)* dealt with the dangers faced by German bomber crews operating over the three northern-most counties of England.

During the course of my researches I have acquired a large number of photographs relating to the Teesside area during the 1939-45 period. A number of them are from institutional sources but most are from the family albums of respondents who were kind enough to share them with me.

Some of those pictures appeared in my 1989 publication but this current volume adds to that collection and provides, I hope, a broader glimpse into those dangerous—and occasionally exciting—times when ordinary people were often called upon to do extraordinary things.

Thanks are extended to those who generously gave me permission to use their photographs, as well as to HarperCollins Publishers for permission to quote from Tom Sawyer's *Only Owls and Bloody Fools Fly at Night* (1982) and Peter Stahl's *The Diving Eagle* (1984). The sources of such written material and photographs are acknowledged throughout the book. Ownership of copyright has been credited in all cases where it is known.

Bill Norman
Guisborough, 2004

ENTERTAINMENTS PAGE

ELITE

OPEN DAILY FROM 1-30 p.m.

2 BIG PICTURES

EXCITEMENT WITH THE SILENCERS OFF!

HUMPHREY
BOGART

KAY
FRANCIS

in

**KING OF THE
UNDERWORLD**

(A)

1-40   4-25   7-10   9-45

THEY'LL SLAY YOU WITH LAUGHS!

MARTHA
RAYE — BOB
HOPE

in **NEVER SAY DIE** (U)

2-55   5-40   8-15

REGENT   PALLADIUM

MIDDLESBROUGH.

MONDAY, TUESDAY, WEDNESDAY:

THE RITZ BROS.

in

**THE GOLDWYN
FOLLIES** (U)

with EDGAR BERGEN and CHARLIE
McCARTHY
In Glorious Technicolor

THURSDAY, FRIDAY, SATURDAY:

MICKEY ROONEY

in

The Adventures of
HUCKLEBERRY FINN

with WALTER CONNOLLY

MIDDLESBROUGH

6.30. Twice nightly—8.40

MON., TUES., WED. NEXT

EMLYN WILLIAMS and
ANNA KONSTAM in

**THEY DRIVE
BY NIGHT** (A)

THURS., FRI. & SAT. NEXT

Mischa Auer, Mary Boland,
Edward Everett Horton in

**LITTLE TOUGH
GUYS IN SOCIETY** (U)

All Seats Bookable   Phone 3513

REGENT · REDCAR

TO-MORROW (SUNDAY), at 8 p.m.   PRICES 2/-, 1/6, 1/-   NO BOOKING FEE

RADIO'S ACE VOCALIST AND REDCAR'S
MOST POPULAR STAR

MONTE REY

Singing the Popular Songs of These Years
Don't Miss Him

OWEN WALTERS

and his FULL ORCHESTRA of
12 Performers

with Don Wilson—Leslie Prowe—Al Davis
Ellen Bartley

SEPTEMBER 4th.—Three Days Only—Wallace Beery, Loraine Day in SERGEANT
MADDEN.   SEPTEMBER 7th—Victor McLaglen, Chester Morris, Wendy Barrie in
PACIFIC LINER.

THE PLAZA, Stockton

6.0—Continuous—10.45

MONDAY NEXT

ANNA STEN and ALAN MARSHALL in

EXILE EXPRESS

A beautiful alien called from a land she has learned to love
With WALTER CATLETT AND JED PROUTY
Also Leon Ames and Jean Woodbury in CIPHER BUREAU.
Thursday: TRANSATLANTIC MERRY-GO-ROUND

REGAL Stockton Tel. 66737.

MONDAY, September 4 1939
ALL THE WEEK

**Basil Rathbone
Boris Karloff**

in

**SON OF
FRANKENSTEIN**

At:— 3-20   6-15   9-9

Also

GLENDA FARRELL in

EXPOSED

At:— 2-8   5-3   7-58

4

Cinema entertainment on Teesside
on the week-end that war was declared.

February, 1939. Fear of gas attacks by enemy aircraft prompted the government to issue some 38 million gas masks at the time of the Munich crisis, in September 1938. In Middlesbrough, 100,000 respirators were assembled and distributed by voluntary labour in the space of five days. Distribution of the town's gas mask cartons began in February 1939. Distribution usually took place at the blue-painted police boxes that were dotted around the town. The picture below shows Middlesbrough PC 140 George Gibson performing his duties at the police box that used to be located at the junction of Southfield Road and Woodlands Road. The recipients are Air Raid Precautions' (ARP) wardens, whose job it was to deliver the cartons to households. In addition to distribution, the wardens ensured that the correct sizes had been allocated to individuals and that the masks fitted properly; they also compiled details of surplus masks in households or noted the need for more.

[Photo.*Mrs J. Thornton*]

September, 1939. The construction of trench shelters gets underway at the Marsh Road recreation ground, Middlesbrough (left) while Corporation workmen begin work on similar projects (below) on Clairville Common, near to the junction of Marton Road and the Longlands. [Photo. *Cleveland County Libraries*]

Developments in aviation, particularly during the 1920s and 1930s, had ensured that in any future international conflict every citizen would be a potential target. As early as June 1937, the government was sufficiently alarmed by the international situation to inform local authorities of the importance of making the necessary arrangements to provide for the safety of the civilian population in the event of war breaking out. Middlesbrough's Air Raid Precautions' Committee ultimately provided communal shelters for some 80% (c. 100,000 places) of the town's population, the programme being started in September 1939, when the Munich crisis gave particular impetus.

7

Bernhard Hochstuhl (2nd left) and Eugen Lange(right) arrive in London.
[Photo. *Author's collection*]

The survivors spent two precarious nights at sea—bitterly cold, without sleep, and at all times paddling with their hands to keep their craft head-on to the rough sea. They eventually made landfall at the foot of cliffs one mile north of Sandsend station. By then, Lange was suffering from exposure and nearly unconscious and it was left to Hochstuhl , who was also near to exhaustion, to scale the cliffs and seek help. He was arrested near the entrance to Sandsend railway tunnel by George Thomas, an LNER Special Constable, who took him to the railway station before organising Lange's rescue.

George Thomas (left) and Frank Dring c. 1979. [Photo.*G. Thomas Jnr*]

October 1939. On the afternoon of 17 October, 1939, three Spitfires of No.41 Squadron, Catterick, shot down a Heinkel 111 of the *2nd Staffel* of *Fernaufklärunsgruppe 122* [2.(F)/122], that was on a reconnaissance mission to the Firth of Forth to locate the battle-cruiser HMS *Hood*.

The Heinkel 'ditched' in the North Sea, some 25 miles east of Whitby: two of the crew of four were already dead when the aircraft hit the water. The two survivors, *Unteroffiziers* Bernhard Hochstuhl (wireless operator) and Eugen Lange (pilot), managed to scramble into their rubber boat seconds before the plane sank, taking with it the food and drink they had hoped would sustain them until rescue.

Lange's rescue was carried out by George Thomas, Jack Barker (the Lythe duty constable) and Frank Dring, a Sandsend painter. Using the deflated dinghy as a stretcher, and with Frank Dring *underneath* it to prevent the dinghy from swaying so much that it might unbalance them and send them all crashing below, they pulled, clawed—and occasionally crawled—their way to the top. It was a difficult climb!

After a short stay in Whitby hospital, Lange and Hochstuhl, the *first Germans to be captured on English soil during the Second World War,* were transferred to London for interrogation before being shipped to Canada, where they spent the rest of the war.

In 1979, the two Germans re-visited Sandsend and Whitby on the fortieth anniversary of their rescue, when they were reunited with their rescuers and those who had nursed them back to health. The only person not present was George Thomas: he had died six months earlier. His son took his place.

Above. Forty years on. Eugen Lange (left) and Bernhard Hochstuhl revisit the site of their rescue on 19 October 1939. [Photo. *courtesy of the Whitby Gazette*]

Left. Bernhard Hochstuhl is carried from Whitby Hospital to a waiting car and ultimate internment for the duration of hostilities. [Photo. *Author's collection.*]

1939 was a time for marching. Here we see Great Ayton's fire auxiliaries parading through the village, with members of the British Legion bringing up the rear. Maurice Heavisides leads, followed by (L—R) Wilf Bickerton, Billy Teasdale and George Hoggart. [Photo. *M Heavisides*]

8 November 1939. The late-afternoon scene at 97 Cambridge Road, Linthorpe, Middlesbrough, shortly after a Lockheed Hudson aircraft (serial N7290) of No. 220 Squadron (Coastal Command), Thornaby, had struck the roof and fallen into the front garden.

The aircraft, piloted by Pilot Officer Augustus Ryan, was on a landing approach to the aerodrome and at an altitude of 600 feet when an engine stalled. The circumstances immediately prior to the crash are unclear: one witness claimed that there was nothing to indicate that the plane was in difficulties before it fell; others claimed that an Auxiliary Fire Service crew out on other duties had seen the aircraft apparently in difficulties and had followed, just in case. Certainly the emergency services were very quickly on the scene and were thus able to deal with the three houses that had been set on fire.

The crash caused no civilian casualties—the house occupants were in the back of the property and thus escaped injury—but Ryan and his crew (Sergeant Rex Mitchell and Aircraftman Albert Wade), together with their passenger (Pilot Officer Douglas Robertson), were killed. [Photo. *Author's collection*]

Pilots of the R.A.F. . . . . . .

September 1939. Barrage Balloon over ICI Billingham [Photo. *courtesy of ICI*]

'commando' raid quite early on in any conflict.

The plant was one of the first locations in the country to be given balloon cordon protection and the plant was extensively camouflaged. Additional defence measures included anti-aircraft guns, as well as RAF fighter squadrons at the already established airfields at Catterick and Usworth. Eight decoy sites were also constructed in the vicinity in the hope of deceiving night bombers (see pages 60-62).

The Billingham plant was the target for German bombers on eleven occasions between June 1940 and July 1942 and 106 high explosive bombs and a large number of incendiaries fell inside the works' perimeter. However, damage was viewed as 'light'

Six of the raids were classed as major, but no vital part of the plant was ever hit. The most spectacular bombing incident occurred in July 1942, when 1,000,000 gallons of petrol were lost in a fire following destruction of some of the storage tanks at the riverside oil jetty site (see page 81)

September, 1939. The ICI plant at Billingham was considered to be the country's most important chemical factory and was expected to be one of the Luftwaffe's first targets in the event of war.

When war was declared in September 1939, the plant was already well established as a key producer of agricultural fertilisers, raw materials for the manufacture of explosives, hydrogen gas for barrage balloons, and high-octane synthetic spirit. In the summer of 1940, the firm's engineering workshops also began the manufacture of aero-engine parts and, subsequently, a wide range of armaments, including mortars and anti-tank weapons.

A number of military authorities were doubtful that the works could be adequately defended against air attack and there were even those who thought that it might be the subject of a German

September 1939. ICI's main offices and parts of the plant already under camouflage. [Photo: *courtesy of ICI*]

During the 1939-45 period most commercial vehicle production went to the armed forces, with only a limited number of small– to medium-capacity vehicles being made available to the Fire Service and to Civil Defence authorities.

Perhaps in anticipation of the likely shortage of fire-fighting appliances in the event of war, the Home Office had distributed trailer pumps to brigades prior to the conflict and these could be pulled by *any* vehicle to which towing equipment had been fitted.

Many large cars were thus adapted for use as emergency fire-fighting units. Other, larger, private cars with a long wheelbase also had the body removed from a point just behind the front doors and an ambulance body fitted.

The men of the Great Ayton fire crew had a Ford V8 towing unit : a saloon car chassis with the rear of the body removed and a van body fabricated to carry the crew on two longitudinal seats. Two ladders were carried on the roof and small items of equipment were stowed within the body.

c. 1942. Great Ayton fire-fighters practise their skills under the leadership of Maurice Heavisides (first left) in the hills behind the village. [Photo. *M. Heavisides*]

c.1940. Whenever residents of the Billingham Urban District Council area had to be transported to hospital during the Second World War, it tended to be done in some style—in the back of the Rolls Royce shown here, the tail-gate being lowered to accommodate stretcher and patient.

Although it was not unusual for Authorities to commandeer private vehicles for emergency services during the war, the Rolls Royce did not come into that category.

In the Billingham UDC area it was members of the Fire Brigade who staffed the ambulance service before the war and they continued to do so during the conflict. The Rolls had been in regular use by the Brigade long before the deterioration of the international situation and, indeed, it continued to be so after the German surrender and until the introduction of the National Health Service.

In the picture above, Billingham firemen pose with their pride and joy; the photograph on the right shows a young patient ready to be loaded on board—and gives new meaning to the term 'tail-gating'. [Photo. *J.P. Richmond,*]

Three of Saltburn's civil defence units ready for action! It is believed that all three photographs were taken on the same (unknown) date, perhaps on a training exercise somewhere on the coastal strip between Redcar and Saltburn.

The pictures feature Sections from the Auxiliary Fire Service (AFS), the Anti-Gassing Service and the Rescue Service and show an interesting array of vehicles that, presumably, were requisitioned and pressed into service for civil defence needs. Unfortunately, the date of the photographs is unknown and the men have not been identified.

Note the white-painted bumper bars and the hooded headlamps, which indicate that Blackout Regulations are in operation. [Photos. *John Grant,*]

1940. The possibility of invasion of this country by the Germans was very real in the summer of 1940. In military circles there were those who believed that if the nation's defensive forces—such as they were—were pushed back from the coast, specially prepared light forces should be left behind to harass the invader's further advance. Thus the idea of British *Maquis* movement was born.

It was not long before a secret Resistance organisation, military in character, had been created behind the main defences that were beginning to change the coastal landscape from Pembroke to Dumfries. The new organisation, known as the Auxiliary Unit, was made up of small 'patrols' of seven or eight men who were to operate in their home areas. Each member was specially selected from local Home Guard volunteers in towns and villages along the eastern and southern coastal areas of Britain. The Unit was organised into three broad geographical locations and numbered accordingly: Auxiliary Unit 201 was located in Scotland, 203 was located in the south of England, and 202 looked after the middle section. The Teesside patrols belonged to Auxiliary Unit 202.

In their earliest days, the Auxiliary Units were envisaged as being expendable: soon after their area had been over-run by invaders, they were to emerge from their hiding places and inflict as much damage as possible on the enemy before either being killed or making their way back to British lines. The risks would certainly be high if the volunteers were called upon—and yet those responsible for recruiting men for local patrols had no difficulty in finding suitable men willing to take the risk.

The members of each patrol were sworn to total secrecy—excluding even their families from the knowledge—and contacts with the Home Guard were severed, although the uniform continued to be worn in order to preserve the illusion of normality.

Having severed links with their original unit, they trained only with members of their own group. Gun-firing practice was carried in local gravel pits or quarries and the men were given unlimited access to available arms (revolvers, rifles, Thompson sub-machine guns) much to the chagrin of Home Guard colleagues who might be training with sticks because of the shortage of weapons.

Instruction was given in the use of explosives, the arts of sabotage and—after training at the Coleshill Warfare Centre, Coleshill, Wiltshire—the more lethal aspects of unarmed combat. Training that required secrecy was carried out in members' homes under the guise of 'Home Guard' business to keep the truth from families.

Night exercises were a common feature, the trainees being set against forewarned regular troops in order to perfect the skills of orientation, infiltration and evasion. Sometimes they moved against designated targets, such as Goosepool aerodrome (now Teesside airport) or Wynyard Hall, which in those days was a military HQ. Percy Bell, a 202 Sergeant with the Bishopton (near Sedgefield) patrol remembered '... *that just about every lad got into the aircraft storage areas of Goosepool during an exercise early in 1941 and the Station Commander gave his troops a severe dressing down when he found out...*'

The idea that Auxiliary Units were immediately expendable faded when a case was made for constructing underground hide-outs, to be stocked with rations, bedding, stoves, explosives, sabotage equipment and arms. Hidden in these subterranean retreats, it was argued, guerrillas would have a sporting chance, not merely of inflicting one suicidal pin-prick but of remaining a thorn in the side of an enemy for weeks or even months.

Suitable sites were chosen, usually in the countryside and, in great secrecy, teams of Royal Engineers dug out underground chambers big enough to accommodate eight men and lined with planks, or brick or corrugated iron sheets. Entrances were extremely well camouflaged by teams of experts from the Shepperton film studios.

In the early summer of 1940, Ted Dixon was the Yorkshire Insurance Company's Middlesbrough manager and and a member of 202. He was subsequently appointed group commander for the Guisborough area and was responsible for eight patrols, at Stokesley, Ayton, Newton-under-Roseberry, Castleton, Redcar, Grangetown and Eston. He told the author:

'*On balance, because the invasion didn't take place, it was probably all a waste of time and money. But if Jerry had come, it would have been a different matter. I think that we would have been a damn nuisance to him, but we wouldn't have lasted long; we would soon have been traced because we were all local.'*

Happily, 'Jerry' never came, and the men who were willing to take on a dangerous and onerous task when all seemed lost never had to practise their deadly skills. Most of them are now dead, and those who survive tend to be reticent about wartime days. However, their gesture *is* worthy of note.

The author of this book knows of many 202 underground hiding places that still exist in the area around Teesside. These dark and crumbling structures are, in effect, monuments to critical times and bear witness to men who were ready to risk everything to confront a threat which, had it become reality, would have touched us all.

Drawing by Stuart McMillan of a 202 underground 'hide' recently found on Eston Hills. [Photo. *Stuart McMillan*]

Ted Dixon's 202 identity card. [Photo. *Ted Dixon*]

1990. Percy Bell of the Bishopton 202 'patrol.
[Photo. *Stockton & Darlington Times*]

Auxiliary Units' badge.
[Photo. *Author's collection*]

3 February 1940. The wreck of a Heinkel 111 bomber (coded 1H+FM) of the *4th Staffel* of *Kamppfgeschwader 26* (4./KG26) lies behind the cottages at Bannial Flatt Farm, at the Sleights crossroads some four miles north of Whitby.
[Photo. *Author's collection*]

This was the first German aircraft to crash on *English* soil during the Second World War. It was on anti-shipping operations when it was intercepted five miles east of Whitby at 9.40am by three Hurricane fighters of No.43 Squadron, Acklington, Northumberland. Acklington was the only fighter station in the three north-eastern counties not snow-bound that day.

 The bomber was shot down by Flight Lieutenant Peter Townsend (later, Group Captain and Equerry to Queen Elizabeth II) who became famous during the 1950s because of his romantic involvement with Princess Margaret.

 Two members of the Heinkel's crew of four were wounded and two were killed. Townsend visited the wounded members in Whitby the following day and took them oranges and cigarettes—and when the other two were buried at Catterick, with full military honours, there was a wreath and a card 'From 43 Squadron, with sympathy'. The bodies have since been exhumed and re-interred at the German Military Cemetery, Cannock Chase, Staffs.

Left. This maker's plate, 'rescued' from the wreck by a souvenir hunter, shows the aircraft type, its serial number and its year of manufacture.
[Photo. *Author's collection*]

ARADO-Flugzeugwerke
G. m. b. H.
Lizenz: Heinkel, Rostock
Typ HE111H W. Nr. 02323
Abnahmedatum 1938

The crew of the 'Bannial Flatt' Heinkel 111 with their aircraft. **L—R:** *Unteroffizier* Johann Meyer (gunner/mechanic), *Feldwebel* Hermann Wilms (pilot), 3rd is a friend from another crew, *Unteroffizier* Karl Missy (gunner/wireless operator), *Unteroffizier* Rudolf Leushake (observer). Only Missy and Wilms survived the encounter with the Hurricanes. [Photo. *C & N Hegemann*]

April, 1940. On 3 April, 1940, a Spitfire of No. 41 Squadron entered the history books when it became the first RAF fighter to be lost to the Luftwaffe in defence of these shores during the Second World War.

The fighter, flown by Flt/Lt Norman Ryder, had left Greatham airfield (RAF West Hartlepool), where he was on daily detachment from Catterick aerodrome, to intercept a Heinkel 111 bomber (coded 1H+AC) of II./KG26 that was attacking shipping off the North Yorkshire coast. In the ensuing combat, the adversaries shot each down. The Germans were rescued by the Scarborough trawler *Silver Line* and were landed at Scarborough; Ryder was picked up by the Hartlepool trawler *Alaskan* after ditching in rough seas some fifteen miles east of Redcar and was subsequently landed at Hartlepool.

Some time after Ryder's rescue by the *Alaskan*, the pilots of No.41 Squadron presented the boat's skipper, Bill Craske, with an engraved tankard. The momento is now held by his daughter, Mrs Mavis Wright, of Hartlepool.

Some of the crew of *Silver Line* pose with one of the statuettes which were presented to each member of the crew by the Mayor of Scarborough. The awards were in recognition of the crew's part in the rescue on 3 April, 1940. **L—R:** Chas. Hunter, Ted Robinson, Bill Watkinson (skipper), Tom Watkinson, Bob Watkinson (mate). Other members of the crew were A. Barley (engineer), WG Cole (2nd engineer), D. Holmes (cook). [Photo. *via Peter Watkinson*]

Flt/Lt Norman Ryder.
[Photo. *Author's collection*]

The trawler *Silver Line*.
[Photo.*George Scales*]

Bill Craske's tankard. [Photo. *Author*]

PRESENTED
TO
W. E. CRASKE
BY THE
PILOTS OF 41 SQUADRON
TO COMMEMORATE
THE RESCUE OF F/LT. E.N. RYDER
AT SEA ON THE
3RD APRIL 1940

The crew of the Heinkel 111 (1H+AC) of II./KG26. The pilot, *Leutnant* Rudolf Behnisch (centre) renewed his acquaintance with the Watkinson family when he and his wife visited Scarborough in 1990 on the anniversary of his rescue. The crew of *Silver Line* were no longer alive and so the visitors were welcomed by Bob Watkinson jnr and his family. [Photo. *Rudolf Behnisch.*]

There were two CH stations in Yorkshire: one at Staxton Wold, near Bridlington, and one at Danby Beacon. Although this photograph (left) of Danby Beacon CH was taken in the early 1950s, little had changed from wartime days.

There can be little doubt that those two CH stations saved Yorkshire from more damage from raiders than it actually suffered for the operators working there kept track of most hostile planes approaching the area and this enabled fighters to be scrambled to head them off.

Danby's first success came on 3 February 1940, when Hurricane fighters of No. 43 Squadron, Acklington, Nothumberland, were alerted and successfully intercepted a German raider that was subsequently shot down near Whitby.

The station was officially closed down on 30 November, 1945, but it was not until the 1950's that the buildings and the 360 feet-high towers were demolished. [Photo. *Fred Smith*]

1940. Immediately prior to the war, British scientists had hurriedly prepared for service a chain of rudimentary radar stations which, by the summer of 1939, was able to detect aircraft approaching at medium or high level at distances of some 100 miles; these stations were Fighter Command's long-range eyes.

When war was declared, there were eighteen of these radar stations, code-named Chain Home (CH), in operation and giving interlocking cover along the eastern and southern coats of Britain between Portsmouth and Aberdeen. The term 'radar' (**RA**dio **D**etection **A**nd **R**anging) was not coined until after the Americans entered the war in 1941. Prior to that, the system was known as 'RDF' (**R**adio **D**irection and **F**inding).

Memorial plaque at the site of the radar station at Danby Beacon.
[Photo. *Author*]

April, 1940. When the Minister of Agriculture coined the phrase 'Dig for Victory' on 4 October 1939, he was addressing not only farmers but also everyone who had a garden. The ultimate aim was to make Britain self-sufficient in food. To that end, arable farming was extended at the expense of pastoral, and householders increased their own output by turning lawns and flower-beds over to the growing of vegetables.

All spare land in towns was also utilised, including this patch adjacent to the Cenotaph outside Albert Park's main gates. In this picture, taken in April 1940, a group of boys from Ayresome Senior School prepare land for potato planting. The Morris car showroom in the background (left) still stands but nowadays it sells Japanese cars. The ground so enthusiastically tilled by the six boys now forms one of the flower-beds that surround the Cenotaph.

Ayresome Senior School pupils digging for victory in April, 1940. [Photo. *E. Baxter/ Evening Gazette*]

May, 1940. The presentation of the first wartime ambulance to the town of Redcar took place at the municipal buildings, Coatham Road, in May 1940. Numbering from L—R, the party includes: Ald. C. Harris (3rd), Mayor J. Coupland (9th), **then** Cllr J. T. Fletcher, Dr. E. Fallows, Mr. H. Caldwell (Town Clerk), J. Welford, Mrs Welford, and Cllr Mrs I. Lonsdale. Note the white bumper and the headlight hood, both fitted to comply with the Blackout Regulations.
[Photo. *courtesy Northern Echo via Kirkleatham Museum*]

NOTICE TO THE INHABITANTS OF THE PARISHES OF EGTON & GLAISDALE.

In the event of a hostile landing or Bombardment your attention is drawn to the Lord Lieutenant's Circular, issued to every householder.

Local guides (wearing green bands) or Motor Cyclists will probably give notice of the enemy landing in the district.

Special Constables (wearing white bands on their left arms) will proceed to their allotted station to help the inhabitants, and do work which has been assigned to them.

All people are advised to get fully dressed in as warm clothing as possible, with over coat and blanket rolled up, and collect prepared food, such as they can carry in readiness to move where required.

In the unlikely event of orders being given by the Military to leave the villages and farms in order to proceed inland, people will be told off to see that any persons unable to walk are placed in the first available vehicles.

The inhabitants of Egton should proceed to Egton Bridge, and by the Moor Roads to Rosedale and Pickering, via. Stape.

The inhabitants of Glaisdale, Egton Banks, and Shortwaite will go up the dale and beyond.

The inhabitants of Lealholm will go inland, via. Fryup and Cock Heads. Assistance will be given up the Banks, if possible, by men and horses.

The Guisborough High Road and York High Road (after a couple of hours) are reserved for the Soldiers, and cannot be used.

Special Constables will be placed at Cross Roads and other important places to give directions and generally help. They must be implicitly obeyed, and they have orders to remain at their posts until all have started.

On no account are the inhabitants to carry any arms whatever, as the mere fact of doing so would be used as an excuse for killing everyone as in Belgium.

A limited number of trains may or may not be available on the North Eastern Line, probably not.

On special orders being given by the Military, Farmers must kill, or drive their cattle into Egton Bridge, Glaisdale, or Fryup, as the case may be, having first sent off as many women and children as possible in their carts and waggons.

It is advisable that carts and waggons should contain some straw, blankets, food, thick clothes, and food for the horses.

In the event of bombs being dropped from the air or shells firing, people are earnestly advised to seek shelter in cellars, or in rooms on the ground floor. They are on no account to proceed into streets, or expose themselves on roads.

N.B.—The object of these instructions is the prevention of panic. The preservation of life, not property, therefore the people should be discouraged from carrying anything but food and blankets.

J. KENNETH FOSTER,
Member of the Emergency Committee.

NEWTON AND SON, PRINTERS, WHITBY.

1940—when the expectation of invasion was clearly very real

September 1940. Films on offer at Teesside cinemas during the week commencing 9 September 1940 included those shown here. Given the country's predicament in 1940, one cannot help but feel that the film on show at the *Empire* was nearer to the truth than that being offered at the *Globe*.

Opposite page. HQ Company, 8th Battalion Green Howards (Home Guard)whose base was the drill hall in Bright Street, Middlesbrough.
[Photo. *George Perkins,*.]

In mid-May, 1940, as the German advance through France continued and fears of invasion grew, Anthony Eden, Secretary of State for War, broadcast to the men of Britain to form units of Local Defence Volunteers (LDV). The appeal offered an opportunity to those who, because of age or work, could not join the Services but who wanted to 'hit back'.

Within twenty-four hours 250,000 men had answered the call and that number had grown to 1,000,000 by 23 July when, at Churchill's suggestion, the LDV was re-named Home Guard. Middlesbrough formed two battalions, the 37th and the 60th. On 25 January 1941, they became the 8th and 9th North Riding(Middlesbrough)Battalions, respectively, and Green Howards' badges were distributed.

Participation was voluntary and unpaid but a uniform and a rifle were provided free of charge. Provision of the latter often took some time: when George Coupland of Dormanstown joined at Warrenby works in 1940 he had to go on patrol of the works armed only with a stick! Later, he was provided with a 12-bore shot-gun—without ammunition—and used to rattle the bolt to scare those people he had to challenge during the hours of darkness.

Each large industrial unit had its own defence contingent, drawn from employees. Their task was to guard the premises during the hours of darkness—and often after a day's work—while the danger of invasion existed. As the threat receded, many Home Guard units trained for local anti-aircraft defence. The Middlesbrough contingents first manned the town's ack-ack defences on the night of 6-7 July, 1942, when the town was raided by the Luftwaffe bomber unit *Kampfgeschwader 2* (KG2).

The last parade of local Home Guard units took place on 4 December, 1944, when it was noted that 23,000 officers and men had served in the Tees' garrison, including 3,500 who had served continuously since volunteering in 1940.

HQ Company, 8th Battallion, Green Howards (Home Guard), whose base was at the drill hall, Bright Street, Middlesbrough.
[Photo. *George Perkins*]

Marske and Redcar the Stray saw an accumulation of concrete strong points (known as 'pillboxes'), machine-gun posts and searchlight emplacements, while in fields off Green Lane the guns of an anti-aircraft battery pointed skywards.

Further inland, road signs were removed and road barriers were set up throughout the area (and the nation); pillboxes were constructed at strategic locations and large blocks of concrete were set down as tank traps in any location considered to be vulnerable.

This undated war-time photograph (left) of Redcar sea front has a depressive air about it: the sand-bags, the shuttered amusement palaces and cafés, and the barbed-wire all combine to give the resort a grim countenance.

[Photo. *Author's collection*]

1940. In the summer of 1940, the strong belief that the invasion of this country was imminent prompted the authorities to take measures which they hoped would hinder the progress of an enemy.

Cleveland's coastal fringe was mined with explosives and the beaches were littered with concrete blocks, steel spikes and barbed wire to obstruct the movement of enemy personnel and vehicles that might be landed from the sea. At both Saltburn and Redcar, the military authorities closed the piers to general use and dismantled parts of them to prevent their possible use by an invader; barbed wire stretched from the river Tees to Saltburn; and between

Military artefacts dating from the Second World War can still be found dotted around the Teesside landscape. These pictures show three examples of pillboxes at the South Gare (above), at Yarm (right) and at Skinningrove (upper right, as it was in 1990)
[All photos. *Author*]

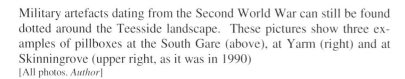

1940. The retained fire crew of Stokesley's Fire Brigade pose alongside their Morris Commercial appliance in T. Durham's farmyard. where the machine was kept.
Front (L—R): J. Jackson, J. Coulson, W. King, G. Dobson, C. Smith, R. Walshaw, J. Durham, T. Durham, G. Hallworth, L. Armstrong, R. Chapman and C. Moon.
Back (L—R): A. Johnson, R. Borthwick, P. Leng, S. Swales, B. Armstrong, W. Kearsley, N. Percival, and J. Lilystone. [Photo. *George Perkins*]

1940.   Stokesley retained fireman, J. Coulson, stands with extinguisher at the ready as he poses with the Brigade's Morris Commercial appliance. Note the hooded headlight, a condition imposed by the wartime Blackout Regulations for all vehicles.   The purpose of such devices was to ensure that the feeble light that was allowed to illuminate the vehicle's nocturnal progress was not spotted by enemy aircraft and so become an aiming point for bombs.
[Photo. *George Perkins*]

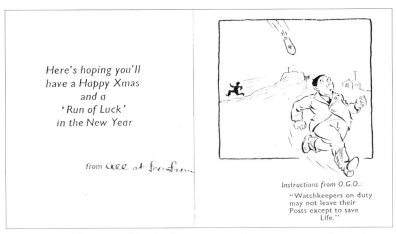

Here's hoping you'll
have a Happy Xmas
and a
'Run of Luck'
in the New Year

from *all at Hinderwell*

Instructions from O.G.O.:
"Watchkeepers on duty
may not leave their
Posts except to save
Life."

There were still opportunities for humour, even in the most dire circumstances. This Royal Observer Corps (No.9 Group, York) Christmas card depicts duty observers following Corps instructons to the letter. The card shown above is a copy of one sent by Leo Welford, of Hinderwell, to his friend and colleague Fred Askew, a Whitby observer. [Photo. A. Askew]

Opposite page. There were at least thirteen Observation Corps posts in the Teesside/Cleveland area. Their aim was to ensure the accurate identification of aircraft - both friendly and hostile - overflying specified areas. The posts included sites at Eaglescliffe, Eston, Redcar, Seaton Carew, West Hartlepool, Loftus, Hinderwell, Castleton, Great Ayton, Newton Bewley and Saltburn.

Posts were usually located in elevated spots off the beaten track and initially consisted of little more than a circle of layered sandbags with an inner circle of corrugated iron. In the early days, a spluttering stove and the sandbags were the only protection against inclement weather. Each post was manned by two men at all times, each pair completing a 'watch' of four hours. All were volunteers, though some were full-timers and others worked part-time, and were drawn from a variety of occupations. Each received 1s 3d (5½p) per hour, the full-timers working a 48-hour week.

When an aircraft was detected by sight or by sound, its height and direction of flight were determined and its position 'fixed' on a plotting table. The information was then passed to all other posts in the neighbourhood. Details were also transmitted to the regional Fighter Command HQ for appropriate action. Once an incoming aircraft crossed the coast, its position was passed from post to post so that the aircraft was never 'lost'.

The Redcar post had a 'special' observer among its personnel: 'Paddy', a smooth-haired fox-terrier belonging to W.R. Vincent, the head observer, developed an uncanny accuracy in detecting approaching hostile aircraft.

The dog would prick up its ears when a faint drone was heard and would listen intently. Then it would either settle down or 'walk about in a bustling sort of way'. Whenever the dog 'bustled', the drone usually came from a raider.

Members of the 03/9 Royal Observer Corps unit, Hinderwell, in June 1945. Those pictured are (left - right). *Back row:* Mr Goldstraw, Leo Welford, Tom Jefferson, Ronnie Toes, Bill Welford, Alan Grainger, Bill White, Mr Wilks. *Middle row:* George Foster, Joe Dawson, George Sherwood, Gibson Jefferson, Harry Heseltine. *Front row:* Herman Wood, Reg Barrett, Captain Codling, Harold Featherstone, Percy Tawn, Willie Harrison, Bob Sanderson. [Photo. *Ms T. Wilkinson*]

1940. Auxiliary Fire Service (AFS) Section Officer Stan Haggarth sits astride his motorcycle outside his 'action station', which stood opposite the east end of Nelson Street, South Bank. On nationalisation of the AFS to the National Fire Service (NFS) in 1941, the station became known as 2Y of 'A' Division (Middlesbrough) of No.2 Fire Force.

Note the adherence to Blackout Regulations: the white-tipped front mudguard and also the masked headlamp, the 'beam' from which was restricted to the size of the centre hole cut into the masking material. Note also that in the background the Ford V8, which was used to pull a Sigmond trailer pump, also has hooded headlamps. The layers of sandbags against the building were placed there as protection against blast in the event of an air raid on the locality

Also in the picture, from L—R are: Tommy Jamieson, S. Ainsworth, and Albert Peacock. Peacock was the owner of the black and white terrier, called 'Spot', that can be seen alongside the front of the car.

Apparently, 'Spot' used to race after the team on every call-out. Stan maintains that although the dog could not keep up with the V8, the animal always turned up at the scene of the fire—often after having taken a number of short cuts en route! [Photo. *Stan Haggarth.*]

c. 1940. Newport Road, looking towards Corporation Road. To the right stands Binns department store, which was spectacularly destroyed by fire in March, 1942, and had to be demolished.. A more recent structure now occupies the site. Alongside it is the *Grand Electric* cinema with its glittering lower façadé of green Bakerlite edged with chrome.

Fondly remembered by children of the 1940s/1950s as the location of so many Saturday morning triumphs of cowboy heroes—Roy Rogers, Gene Autrey, The Durango Kid—the 'Electric' showed its last film on 8 April, 1961, before being demolished to make way for shops and Gas Board showrooms.

During the subsequent decades, the pace of re-development accelerated and most of the buildings shown in this photograph followed the *Grand Electric* into oblivion.
[Photo. *Author's collection*]

GRAND ELECTRIC THEATRE   Middlesbrough.
ALL NEXT WEEK.

The RITZ BROTHERS in **THE GORILLA** (H). | Also PRESTON FOSTER in **CHASING DANGER** (U)

Children under 16 not admitted, whether accompanied by adults or not.

In Middlesbrough, the principal target area for the bombs of the Luftwaffe must surely have been the Ironmasters' District, which occupied that rough triangle of land on the south side of the Tees' loop between the Newport and Transporter bridges.

Not only did the site embrace the Acklam and Britannia group of iron and steelworks of Gjers' Mills and Dorman Long, the north bank of the river provided the location of the Furness shipyards at Haverton Hill (upper right) and the ICI chemical plant at Billingham (upper left).

However, in spite of this concentration, it would seem that it was only on relatively rare occasions that such industrial targets were hit during air raids. Even then, damage tended to be light. More often than not, bombs intended for the Ironmasters' District fell in open country or they fell—with tragic consequences—on the working class residential areas that fringed the southern edge of the railway from Newport to Albert Road.

Midlesbrough's Ironmasters' District [Photo. *Author's collection*]

The Ironmasters' District effectively masked by industrial smoke and haze. [Photo. *Author's collection*]

Later generations were to denounce such atmospheric pollution as being injurious to health, but during wartime there were those who believed that such emissions provided a protective screen that made accurate bombing difficult and were largely responsible for many bombs going astray and exploding in open country.

Early in 1941, such 'normal' emissions were supplemented by the distribution of hundreds of oil-burning furnaces—'like tar machines'—which were spaced at intervals along road-side kerbs at strategic points around the town, especially in close proximity to important industrial establishments, such as ICI Billingham.

When a raid was impending, it was the responsibility of the Pioneer Corps, acting under the Ministry of Home Security, to ignite the furnaces in specified locations, dependent upon wind direction. As they burned, the fires produced large volumes of dense, black smoke to screen the town from raiders. When there were '...*smoke wagons all along Cannon Street...the*

air..used to be absolutely thick...' On one occasion, the furnaces issued their palls of smoke over a wide area of Teesside for thirteen nights in succession. '*Everything was blacked out and people found difficulty finding their way home. The objectionable smell permeated everything and found its way into houses, even though every crevice in doors and windows had been plugged with paper or rages.*'

Mayor (centre), Miss Batten (on the Mayor's right),
Captain Slinn, Ald. A. Sadler and Cllr H. French (left)

During her visit, Miss Batten confessed that she found ambulance driving rather unexciting but that she expected it would become pretty lively when the group reached France. In the light of subsequent events, perhaps it became too lively!

In May, 1940, the Corps had a unit of twenty-two fully equipped ambulances in France and another twenty-two almost ready for shipment. It was hoped that other vehicles on order would soon bring the total strength to 110 vehicles in a very short time. Over fifty towns in the country had undertaken to provide and equip such vehicles. Following the visit, the Mayor decided to present a fully equipped vehicle in the name of the town to the Corps, while in Stockton the Mayor and Mayoress, Ald. And Mrs J. W. Gargate, instigated a fund to do the same. [Photo. *E. Baxter/Evening Gazette*]

May, 1940. On Friday, 24 May, 1940, a fleet of six ambulances belonging to the Anglo-French Ambulance Corps called at Middlesbrough and Stockton.

The vehicles, which had been presented to the Corps by the Durham Mineworkers' Federation for service in France and at a cost of £500 each, were en-route to Durham in the charge of Corps Adjutant B. T. Slinn. In Durham they were formerly handed over to the Corps by David Grenfell, MP.

When the Mayor of Middlesbrough, Cllr Sir William Crosthwaite, inspected the fleet he met Miss Jean Batten (the famous airwoman who had achieved fame with her record-breaking Australia—England flights during the 1930s) who had recently joined the Corps.

The photograph (left) shows a group at the inspection and includes the

Jean Batten
[Photo. *Author's collection*]

40

Zielstammkarte

Land: Großbritannien
England (Yorkshire)

Ort: Middlesbrough

(Nähere Lage) am rechten Ufer des River Tees, etwa 500 m im O des Hauptbahnhofs.

Geogr. Werte:
54°34'35" N
1°13'14" W

Ziel-Nr. G.B. 45 10
mit G.B. 61 10

Kartenbl.-Nr. E 6/1:100 000

C. B. Nr. E 15/1:63 360

1. Bezeichnung des Zieles:

Hafenanlagen.
Chemische Werke "Sadler & Co. Ltd.".

Vgl. mit Ziel-Nr. G.B. 61 1 Teerdestillationsanlage "Clarence Works", 0,9 km im NO.

2. Bedeutung:

Middlesbrough ist Haupteinfuhrhafen für Eisenerze.
Die Ausfuhr besteht aus Eisen- und Stahlwaren, Maschinen
sowie Produkten der Kokerei- und chemischen Industrie.

3. Beschreibung des Zieles: Höhe über NN: 5 m.

a) Verkehrsanschlüsse: Straßenverbindung, Wasseranschluß über River Tees zur Nordsee.
Eigener Gleisansanschluß. Nächster Bahnhof Middlesbrough
Hauptbahnhof (500 m im W).

b) Ausdehnung insgesamt: Etwa 385 000 qm.   Bebaute Fläche: Etwa 20 000 qm.
W-O etwa 1100 m
N-S etwa 900 m.

Part of a Luftwaffe target card detailing aspects of Middlesbrough's port installations, Sadler's chemical works and the tar distillation plant at Port Clarence. [Photo. *Author's collection*]

The German Air Force had numerous maps, aerial photographs and models of the Tees area. Such aids to orientation were supplemented by documents such as the one shown here, which gave a complete breakdown of each building on any particular target site, to the extent that dimensions and functions were listed.

Documents in the writer's possession show every potential target of industrial and commercial importance in the Tees area and each group of documents pin-points specific units and buildings within each complex.

The Tees area was not exceptional with regard to such detailed analysis: it simply mirrored the national coverage that the Germans had embarked upon before the outbreak of war.

Much of the information came from Ordnance Survey maps, picture postcards, trade publications and the annual accounts of industrial and trade performance, all of which had been freely available from shops and libraries in Britain before the war. German Intelligence agencies simply drew on all of those sources—and others—and sifted out those that had strategic value.

25 May 1940. Bomb-damaged houses at the rear of Aire Street, South Bank.
[Photo. *Author's collection*]

windows while crossing the railway bridge near the TRTB tram depot (just west of South Bank) when a bomb narrowly missed the bridge and exploded in a field alongside it.

Negligible industrial damage was caused by the raid but there was structural damage to housing in Aire Street, South Bank. There were eight casualties among workmen at the Grangetown plant. This was the first air raid on an industrial target in Britain during the Second World War and it produced the first civilian casualties to arise from a bombing raid on this country during the 1939-45 period.

1940. On the evening of Friday, 24 May 1940, Teddy Jones and his band took a break from their engagement at the Middlesbrough Empire to play at Redcar's Pier Ballroom, where some of the patrons took time off from their dancing to pose for the photograph on the opposite page.

Hours after the picture was taken, the musicians - and possibly some of those shown in the photograph - were passing through South Bank when they were caught up in Teesside's first air raid, in the early hours of 25 May.

Fourteen small calibre bombs fell in a line from Cargo Fleet Ironworks, South Bank, to Dorman, Long's Steelworks at Grangetown. A number of motorists returning home from the dance stopped their cars and dived into ditches when they heard the bombs whistling down. The band's coach suffered broken

Redcar Pier Ballroom, Friday, 24 May, 1940. [Photo. *Jim Cox*]

June 1940. On 10 June, 1940, Mussolini declared war in Germany's favour. Within minutes of the announcement, Middlesbrough police, following Home Office directives, began to round up Italien aliens in the borough.

In the evening of the day of declaration, a hostile crowd of demonstrators toured the streets and attacked six well-known Italian-owned ice-cream parlors and cafés. In Linthorpe Road, Grange Road, Suffield Street, Newport Road and Corporation Road large stones were hurled through plate-glass windows and at shop fronts.

The police took twenty-eight Italian residents between the ages of sixteen and seventy into protective custody and reinforcements of police were stationed in large numbers in the vicinity of establishments bearing Italian names. A number of demonstrators were taken into custody.

On 11 June, police picketed several Italian-owned establishments that had been damaged the night before. One of those was Costantino's, which stood in Newport Road, opposite Newport Crescent and the current Binns store. The site is now occupied by Jessops camera shop.

[Photo.*E.Baxter/Evening Gazette*]

July, 1940. A Heinkel He.59 floatplane of the Luftwaffe air-sea rescue service—the *Seenotflug-kommando*.

An aircraft of this type belonging to *Seenotflugkommando 3* was shot down by three Spitfires of No.72 Squadron, Acklington, in the early morning of 1 July 1940. It force-landed on the sea about four miles east of Hartlepool.

The floatplane was searching for the crew of a mine-laying Heinkel 115 that was missing off the Yorkshire coast. The mine-layer was later found thirty miles off Whitby

During the engagement, the Germans offered no return gunfire and took no evasive action. The German crew of four managed to survive the encounter unscathed and were eventually rescued by the destroyer HMS *Black Swan*. They later protested most strongly about the violation of the Red Cross . It is believed that their aircraft, which was by then in a nose-up vertical position and submerged as far as trailing edge of the wings, was towed to Hartlepool and beached.

Although such air-sea rescue aircraft flew under the protection of the Red Cross, they were believed to be armed and were occasionally seen in the vicinity of British convoys (as the 'Hartlepool' He.59 had been). Therefore, the British Government maintained that, in addition to rescuing downed flyers, such aircraft were reporting shipping movements and were thus involved in activities inconsistent with privileges normally accorded to the Red Cross. Hence, they were fair game in war time. [Photo. *via Ernst Adolf Schneider*]

July, 1940 Clairville Common, Middlesbrough, c. July 1940. A group of shamefaced young schoolboys have just been told that they have violated Defence Regulations!.

In July of that year, the Government decreed that henceforth no kites or balloons were to be flown, except by servants of the King. Seemingly, this was a precaution against illicit signalling by spies.

Whether by accident or design, Ron Yates (left), now of Tiverton, Devon, and some of his pals decided to put the ruling to the test.

They got caught and the photograph shown here was published in the *Evening Gazette* alongside a warning that the flying of kites was prohibited.

Ron confesses that his mother never forgave him for the shame he had brought on the family. How times have changed!

[Photo. *via Ron Yates*]

11 August, 1940. A Ju88A-1 (coded 7A+KH) reconnaissance aircraft of *1 Staffel* of *Fernaufklärungsgruppe 121* [1. (F)/121] after it had belly-landed on Newton Moor, near Scaling Dam.

The aircraft had been on a reconnaissance sortie to the RAF bomber aerodromes of Dishforth and Linton-on-Ouse and was on its way home when it was sighted over Helmsley by three Spitfires of No. 41 Squadron, Catterick.

One member of the crew, *Leutnant* Heinrich Meier, was killed in the air battle that followed. His body was subsequently buried in Acklam Road cemetery, Thornaby and remained there until 1954, when his parents requested its return to Germany.

[Photo. *Author's collection*]

BESATZUNG DER JU88 7A+KH
wurde am 11.8.1940 abgeschossen
und geriet in englische Gefangenschaft.

Left. This commemorative card shows three of the regular crew of Junkers 88 7A+KH and records that they were shot down on 11 August 1940 and taken into captivity. Otto Höfft was the pilot, Hans Marzusch was the observer and Karl-Heiz Hacker was the wireless operator.
[Photo. *via Mel Brown*]

Right. *Leutnant* Heinrich Meier was a communications' specialist assigned to 7A+KH for the trip to Yorkshire. It is believed that his task was to monitor RAF radio frequencies. The operation cost him his life.
[Photo. *Mrs M.. Henderson*]

Men of the Abbey Plain observation post, Whitby, c. 1945. Their post was in a field close to the abbey, which forms the backdrop to the picture. Men of this unit tracked the 'Scaling' Junkers as it passed over Whitby at 15,000 feet on its way in.

Back row (L—R): Jack Page, Norman Schofield, Fred Askew, Joe Harrison (Head Observer), unknown, Harry Clarke, Frank Clarke.
Front row (L__R): W. Ventress, J. Hodgeman, D. Hugill, A Pearson, Alec Urmiston, Stan Wheatley, Percy Burnett, W. Dean.
[Photo. *A. R. Askew,*]

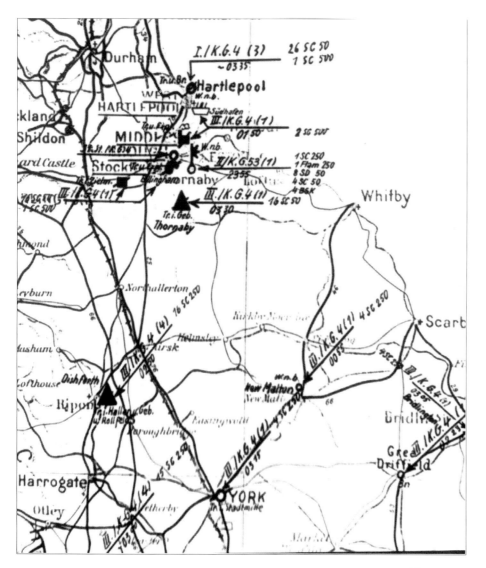

August, 1940. In the early years of the war, at least, the Luftwaffe prepared a detailed operations map for every raid on Britain. The picture (left) shows targets, bomb loads, units involved and times of attack for a series of raids over the Tees area on the night of 24-25 August, 1940. For example, I./KG4 was the unit detailed to attack Hartlepool with three aircraft at 3.35am (German Summer Time, which was two hours in front of Greenwich Mean Time) on 25 August 1940. Those aircraft were detailed to drop twenty-six bombs of 50kg and one bomb of 500kg. The units, targets and bomb loads of all other participant aircraft can be deduced using the same method.

Not all of the aircraft taking part in the raid were of the same type, nor were they from the same airfield. I./KG4 flew Heinkel 111s from Soesterberg (Holland), III./KG4 flew Junkers 88s from Amsterdam/Schipol (Holland), and II./.KG53 flew Heinkel 111s from Lille (France).

Some of the specific targets can be guessed from the map. For example, the attack scheduled for 1.50am (GST) seems to be aimed at Tees power station and Smith's Dock; the 3.30am(GST)raid has Thornaby aerodrome has its target. Unfortunately, all of the other symbols remain a mystery.

Available records show that the sixteen bombs intended for Thornaby aerodrome were dropped at 1.45am Greenwich Mean Time (only five minutes later than planned) but they landed wide of the mark: they fell on open land just to the west of Marton Road and in a line that stretched from Saltersgill Farm to City Road, Belle View.

It is thought that the Germans mistook the open land for the airfield and the straight-running Marton Road as one of the runways. [Photo. *Bundesarchiv*]

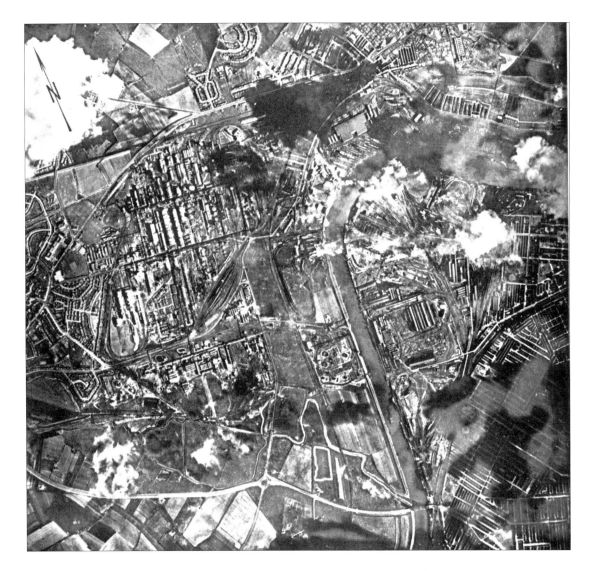

September, 1940. Confirmation of the Luftwaffe's interest in the Ironmasters' District and ICI Billingham.

This Luftwaffe reconnaissance photograph was taken on 14 September 1940. It clearly shows the Ironmasters' District (centre right), the ICI chemical works (centre left), the North Tees power station (left of the lower bend of the river), and the Furness shipyards at Haverton Hill (left of the upper bend of the river). The Tees Bridge at Newport can be seen at bottom right
[Photo.*Imperial War Museum. Neg.MH 29801*]

1940. On Monday evening, 16 September 1940, a German aircraft dropped eight bombs on Whitby. There was considerable damage to property but there were no serious casualties. Properties in Windsor Terrace and the Bobby's Bank area were badly affected and the railway goods' yard was extensively damaged —as can be seen from the photograph. The railway track in the yard was destroyed but local workers ensured that repairs were quickly effected and the line was restored within forty-eight hours.

[Photo. *Doran, Whitby*]

October, 1940. At 7.55pm on Sunday, 13 October 1940, a German aircraft dropped four high-explosive bombs on the Marsh Road area of Middlesbrough and caused severe damage to properties in Benjamin Street, Hatherley Street, Nixon Street, Hartington Street, Marsh Road, Argyle Street, Farrer Street, Jamieson Street and Cannon Street.

In the seconds that it took for those explosions to blast their way through the community, fifteen houses were demolished, thirty-seven were rendered so unsafe that they subsequently had to be demolished, thirty-eight were reduced to a state so unsafe that they had to be evacuated, and a further 100 were badly damaged.   In addition, a further 300 properties sustained damage of a lesser nature.

The material cost was high, but the human cost was higher: twenty dead (of whom four died after admission to hospital), thirty-two seriously injured and seventy-two with minor injuries. A number of people had remarkable escapes that evening, including an ARP worker

and his family of four who had sought the protection offered by the cast iron shelter (left) at the junction of Marsh Road and Farrer Street. When the second bomb landed close to their refuge, the ferocity of the blast blew out both ends of the shelter and catapulted the entire family out of one end. They escaped with scratches: other occupants were killed.

Above. 13 October, 1940. Rescue and demolition parties begin clearance work at 53 Benjamin Street. [Photo. *Teesside Archives*]

Right. The remnants of 168 Marsh Road, the home of 58-year old Mary Emmerson who suffered fatal injuries and later died in the North Riding Infirmary. [Photo. *Teesside Archives,*]

Left. RAF salvage crew at the wreck of Ju88 4D+TS of 8./KG30
[Photo. *Author's collection*]

Below. Gerhard Pohling, gunner/ mechanic of Ju.88 4D+TS.
[Photo. *Author's collection*]

November, 1940. The burnt out wreck of a Junkers 88 bomber (coded 4D+TS) of the *8 Staffel* of *Kampfgeschwader 30* (8./KG30) on the hillside at Glaisdale Head, thirteen miles west of Whitby. The aircraft had been on its way to attack the RAF aerodrome at Linton-on-Ouse when it crashed in the early evening of 1 November 1940, and burst into flames. There were no survivors among the crew of four, who were subsequently buried in Acklam Road cemetery, Thornaby.

The cause of the crash is uncertain. Some claim that mist, seemingly present at the time, may have obscured the pilot's visibility and caused him to strike the rising ground at the head of the dale; others claim that this aircraft may have been the one engaged (and damaged) by anti-aircraft defences at Skinningrove Ironworks as it crossed the coast on its way in.

December 1940. In September, 1940, Alan Deere was a Flight Lieutenant with No.54 (Spitfire)Squadron. He served with great distinction, both during the Battle of Britain and afterwards.

In continuous action from the outbreak of the war until 1943, Deere's official 'score' was: 22 enemy aircraft destroyed; 10 probably destroyed and 18 damaged.

In September,1940, the squadron was 'rested' from the battle that was raging in the south and was posted to Catterick, where it was to operate as a temporary training unit until it returned to the south of England in February, 1941.

Alan Deere was much involved in the training programme—and it almost cost him his life on 28 December, 1940, when his Spitfire was in collision with that of one of his trainees (Sergeant Squires) some 10,000 feet above Crathorne, near Yarm.

Deere landed 400 yards from his aircraft at Town End Farm, Kirklevington. Squires landed at Kirklevington Hall and his aircraft crashed into the banks of the river Leven at Red Hall Farm. Deere recounted the tale in his book *Nine Lives*. (1959).

Above. Alan Deere (front row, 2nd from left) with pilots of No.54 Squadron in 1940. [Photo. A/Cdre *A.C. Deere*].   **Right.** Sergeant Squires.

In September 1987, a team of aviation enthusiasts excavated the site of Deere's Spitfire to a depth of twenty feet to recover numerous items, including the Merlin engine, from the aeroplane once flown by one of the most celebrated pilots of the Battle of Britain.

55

Redcar, Christmas 1940. Alderman C. Harris (Mayor) and his daughter Audrey (Mayoress) attend festivities provided for members of the armed forces by the Redcar Salvation Army. The striking thing about this photograph is the number of grim faces on it. Whether this is a comment on the programme of entertainment provided or upon the (then) international situation is not clear. Alderman Harris was destined not to survive the war: he was killed on the night of 21 October, 1941, when a German bomb struck the Zetland Club, Coatham Road, Redcar. [Photo. *Redcar Library*]

WAR WEAPONS WEEK · MIDDLESBROUGH ·

EEE

ERIMUS

MARCH 8-15

DIARY OF EVENTS

The Mayor extends to YOU an invitation to keep these 'engagements.'

Left. The blacksmith forges £s into armaments during Middlesbrough's War Weapons' Week, 8-15 March, 1941, when the town's War Savings' Committee set itself the target of raising £1,000,000 to finance the building of three destroyers for the Royal Navy.

During that week, RAF bombers showered propaganda leaflets (right) on the town to encourage citizens to finance the war effort through the purchase of War Bonds, Savings Certificates and Savings Stamps.

The dropping of such leaflets was part of a week-long programme of fund raising that included the following attractions: orchestral concerts in the town hall and local cinemas, as well as open-air concerts in a variety of locations around the town; parades by military and civil defence personnel; exhibitions of war artefacts, including captured enemy aircraft and unexploded bombs; an exhibition of war paintings; a military PE display; flying displays by the RAF and displays of gun-drill by local anti-aircraft regiments; window-dressing competitions for local traders; and the showing of publicity films by the National Savings Committee from cinema vans that toured the area.

Middlesbrough War Weapons Week

R.A.F. LEAFLET RAID

THIS MIGHT HAVE BEEN A BOMB!

By courtesy of "Evening Gazette"

LEND FREELY TO POUND HITLER
INSTEAD !

££££££££££££££££££

REDCARS WAR WEAPONS WEEK.

March, 1941. A fanfare greets a procession of civic dignatories, led by a local policeman and headed by the second Marquis of Zetland (right) and the Mayor of Redcar, Ald. C. Harris (left), as they near the platform in the High Street from where the Marquis will declare open the town's War Week. The brick building on the right is the Presbyterian Church; in the background is the *Central* cinema. [Photo. *courtesy of the Northern Echo*]

15 March, 1941. The Newton Memorial Chapel, Loftus, after three high explosives had fallen on Chapel Bank at 4.48am. A further two bombs fell in nearby fields and incendiary bombs fell in fields at Easington, seemingly without effect.

Although the high explosives caused damage to windows over a large area in Loftus, they did not cause serious casualties. The 'Newton' fared less well. After the bombing, it was deemed to be unsafe and was demolished later that year. Two bungalows now occupy the site, which also has a plaque that commemorates the incident. [Photo. *Author's collection*]

A barrage balloon with three of its handlers. Richard Ackroyd (centre), of Hartlepool, spent much of his wartime service manning sites on Seal Sands.
[Photo.*R.Ackroyd,*]

Opposite page. During the course of the Second World War, various forms of decoy were developed on a national scale to confuse enemy bombers and lure bombs to false targets. Such decoys were located in rural areas away from military and strategic establishments but, hopefully, close enough to trick raiders into believing that they were bombing their intended objectives.

Initially, such ruses were used to protect only airfields. However, following the bombing of Coventry in November 1940, the Air Ministry decided to create a decoy network to protect major urban and industrial areas, one of which was Middlesbrough. The decoy located on Sneaton Moor (OS. 94/905002), off the Whitby-Scarborough road some seven miles south of Whitby, was one such site.

Of the type known by the codeword *Starfish,* Sneaton operated at night and consisted of a network of electric lights distributed across five square miles of moor land. The lights simulated street lighting, roof lights, light escaping from open doors, and tram wire flashes. When seen from the air, the effect was of night violations of the wartime black-out. Some parts of the site also had large containers of highly combustible materials that were ignited electrically to provide a variety of fire effects, including those of exploding bombs and flaming eruptions, to simulate a town under air attack.

At ground level, there is little evidence nowadays of the activities once conducted on the moor. Viewed from the ground, all that remains of the elaborate ruse are a number of incomplete curved trenches that casual observers might confuse with a land drainage system. From an altitude of 2,000 feet, the impression is very different and the broken trenches can be seen to form a clear pattern.

It is believed that the trenches were fire-breaks that were used to prevent the uncontrolled spread of the decoy fires during operational use. Eight major circles can easily be seen, as can the tank tracks made sixty years ago when the need for *Starfish* had faded and the training for D-Day was the pressing priority.

When approaching bombers were still way out over the North Sea, the lights were switched on and remained so until the raiders were thought to have seen them. Then they were extinguished in the hope that the *Luftwaffe* had pinpointed their position. When the raiders were overhead, the fires were activated to give the impression of an air raid in progress. If things went according to plan, German bombers on their way to Teesside were duped into bombing the decoy.

The Sneaton site was one of a number protecting Middlesbrough. Four of those [at Dunsdale, Middleton (near Seamer), Osmotherley and above Hutton Village, Guisborough] were controlled by RAF Thornaby. Sneaton was under the direct control of No.80 Wing, Radlett, who issued operational instructions to site personnel by means of a dedicated land line. The site was maintained by personnel from RAF Middleton-St-George, who operated the various devices from a reinforced control bunker some 300-400 yards from the site. There were also a number of decoys on the north side of the river to protect ICI Billingham and the Hartlepools.

The hoax did not always work because Middlesbrough was attacked twelve times during the last war. However, sufficient bombs were scattered around the sites to show that the ruse was effective at least some of the time.

Dickson & Benson have taken this space as a gesture of appreciation to all those who are engaged on A.R.P. work.

DICKSON & BENSON - MIDDLESBROUGH

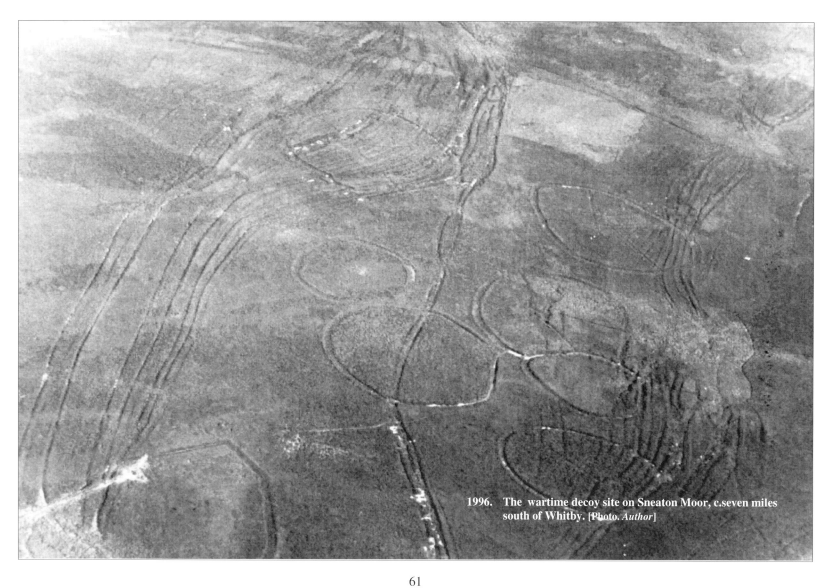

1996. The wartime decoy site on Sneaton Moor, c.seven miles south of Whitby. [Photo. *Author*]

Remnants of decoy sites can still be found around Teesside. The photograph at top left shows the remains of the Dunsdale control bunker, off Sandy Lane; bottom left shows the control bunker at Percy Rigg, above Hutton village, Guisborough.

The photograph above shows the control bunker (left) and air raid shelter (right) at the Greenabella site, which was a decoy for ICI Billingham and was located along the on the Port Clarence—Seaton Carew road.

On the nights of 6 and 7 July, 1942, there were two general attacks which were believed to be directed specifically against ICI. On these occasions, 90% of all bombing was diverted from the factory by Greenabella and other decoy sites in the Port Clarence-Hartlepool area. [Photos. *Author*]

Wartime fashions c. 1940

Right Searchlights over Redcar (date unknown).

There are a number of factors which suggest that this interesting picture is, in fact, a product of 'artistic creation'.

For example, the darkness of the sky is in marked contrast to the brightness of a roadway in sunlight; the apparent unconcern of the pedestrians, suggesting that there is little urgency in the situation; and the angle of the searchlight beams on the right side of the picture—which would place those particular searchlights (and their crews) somewhere in the North Sea!

[Photo. via *George Coupland.*]

Opposite page. In the early years of the war, Britain had virtually no defence against the Luftwaffe's night bombers. Anti-aircraft guns were not particularly effective at shooting down raiders, and we had no efficient night fighter aircraft that could be relied upon to do the job and so night bombers came and went almost as they pleased.

The RAF used Direct Reckoning navigation to strike at targets in Germany. But that method was notoriously inaccurate at night, because of restricted sightings of landmarks to check progress, and so crews did not always arrive at their intended destinations.

The Luftwaffe was far more resourceful. Ground stations in Germany and Occupied Europe transmitted navigational radio beams that were directed over targets in Britain. German night bombers flew along the beams and were thus accurately guided to their targets.

In the early days, the RAF simply tried to 'jam' the beams so that they could not be intercepted by the bombers. But it was soon realized that it would be far better to *mask* the enemy transmission beacon by picking up its beam signal and re-broadcasting it. This masking of the beacons was known as *meaconing*. Horse Close Farm at Marske was a Meacon station, one of seventeen dotted around the country. Marske resident Wilf Priestnall, who was a radio mechanic at Horse Close Farm, explained how it worked:

'The transmitter at Horse Close used to work in conjunction with a receiving station at Brotton, on the site of what is now the Hunley Hall golf course. Brotton picked up the signal coming in from the German transmitter and sent it down to Horse Close Farm by a dedicated land-line. Marske then re-transmitted the signal on the same radio frequency as the German station.

'German aircraft came in following their own beam but then picked up the stronger Marske signal, which they followed (believing that it was their own). The Marske operators slightly shifted the "route" of the original beam signal and in this way the raiders were led away from their intended targets and, hopefully, bombs dropped where they could do little harm.'

The same system was used to confuse Luftwaffe crews returning home over the North Sea after bombing raids. Returning crews used the transmissions of the German beacons as aids for the flight home. But the Marske/Brotton Meacon sent out exactly the same signal as the German station.

If the returning aircraft were nearer to Marske than to its German station, then the aircraft's direction finder gave the bearing for Marske as being the way home. And the crew of the bomber had no way of knowing that this was wrong.

Wilf Priestnall told the author that the system was so secret that the Marske operators were never told of any successes they might have had. However, it is on general record that a number of Luftwaffe crews became hopelessly lost as a result of Meacon activity and crashed in the North Sea or elsewhere when they finally ran out of fuel.

When the Germans realized that their signals were being *meaconed*, they 'hid' their beam signals in transmissions of programmes by the German Broadcasting Service. But when the RAF realized this, Brotton adjusted its receivers, which then automatically picked up such broadcasts and transferred them to Marske for re-transmission.

When Reg Bell lived at Horse Close Farm in the early years of the war, he could never understand why his radio could always pick up the German station *Radio Bremen* far more strongly than it could pick the BBC in London. He always wondered why, but he never learned the reason. If he had been told the truth—that the German broadcasts were being transmitted from the field just over the hedge from his farmhouse—he would not have believed it. And yet it was true. Lord Haw Haw's propaganda programmes were transmitted from Horse Close Farm and it was the RAF that was responsible.

The scattered buildings of the *Meacon* station at Horse Close Farm, Marske, c. 1946. The farmhouse is upper left.
[Photo. *Author's collection*]

Marske's 'Meacon' men c.1942. Wilf Priestnell is 2nd from left, back row. [Photo. *Wilf Priestnell,*]

Artist's impression of the site by Stuart McMillan. [Photo. St*uart McMillan*]

March, 1941. On 30 March, 1941, a Junkers 88 of the *1st Staffel* of *Fernaufklärungsgruppe 123* [1(F)/123] was on an armed photo-reconnaissance sortie to Manchester when it was intercepted over south Durham by two Spitfires, flown by Flight Lieutenant Tony Lovell and Pilot Officer Archie Winskill, of No.41 Squadron, Catterick.

During the course of a short dog-fight over Teesside, eyewitnesses in Redcar saw the Spitfires *'pumping terrific bursts of gunfire'* into their quarry. Minutes later, other eyewitnesses in Normanby saw the fighters chasing the Junkers, which was then *'flying over Eston Hills from the direction of Middlesbrough—but then suddenly it dropped.'* and the chase was over. The Junkers drove deep into the peat on Barnaby Moor, Eston Hills, its explosive impact creating a huge crater and scattering wreckage over a 400 yard radius.

None of the crew of four survived but only one corpse was found. *Unteroffizier* Hans Steigerwald, the Ju88's mechanic/gunner, took to his parachute only moments before his aircraft crashed but he was cruelly served: his parachute failed to open properly and he fell to his death among the trees flanking Flatts Lane, Normanby. He was later buried in Acklam Road Cemetery, Thornaby, where he still lies.

Right. *Uffz.* Hans Steigerwald.
[Photo. *Heinz Steigerwald*]

Upper left. F/Lt Tony Lovell.
[Photo. *via G/Capt. N. Ryder*]

Left. Maker's plate believed to have come from the 'Eston' Ju88.
[Photo. *Author's collection*]

Right. *Feldwebel* (Sergeant) Peter Stahl, a Junkers 88 pilot of the Luftwaffe bomber unit *Kampfgeschwader 30* (KG30), who claimed that he and his crew carried out a lone attack on Middlesbrough on the night of 26-27 April, 1941, after diverting from Hull, which was blanketed by cloud. His bomb load consisted of two parachute mines, one weighing 500kg the other weighing 1,000kg. He described the event thus:

'In the end, I just had to give up (over Hull) *and fly northwards in the hope of finding better visibility. Over Middlesbrough we can finally orientate ourselves beyond question, and I make my bombing run over the town... The AA defences are only moderate, so that we can drop our explosive load quite accurately. On the way out, Hein and Theo report the flaring up of a fire...*

During our return flight over the North Sea I contemplate the sense or otherwise of such attacks. While I can rely on Hans to make every effort to find an important military target for our bombs, I also know that our terrible ammunition may have been unloaded somewhere where it would have no effect at all. Then again, what if it has hit a residential district or even a hospital? This war really is a gruesome business.'

Peter Stahl: *The Diving Eagle*, William Kimber 1984

Existing records make no reference to an attack on the night of 26-27 April—but two separate raids on the Tees' area on the night of 15-16 April 1941, do share common aspects with Stahl's account.

The current writer *knows* that Stahl's dates given in his book (whether by accident or design) are sometimes out by up to fourteen days—just about the same level of discrepancy in the dates for April 1941.

If such a discrepancy is also true in this instance, it seems likely that Stahl's mines fell on Thornaby at c. 2.00am on 16 April. One fell on a derelict industrial unit; the other dropped on the Union Foundry. Industrial buildings were seriously damaged, 140 houses were slightly damaged, a woman 'died of shock' and four people were injured.

Air raid shelters in Laycock Street, Middlesbrough. These brick structures, with roofs of reinforced concrete and with walls strengthened by steel matting, tended to replace the earlier cast-iron surface shelters from 1941 onwards. They were no defence against a direct hit by a bomb but they were certainly more robust than the houses standing alongside them. [Photo. *A. Kirby*]

The brick street shelters would normally withstand the effects of blast—so long as the explosion was not too near. Notice the pock-marked effects of shrapnel. The location of this particular shelter is thought to have been the Foxheads area near Newport bridge, c. May 1941. [Photo. *E. Baxter/Evening Gazette*]

May, 1941. In the early hours of 12 May, 1941, seven high explosives and 'numerous' incendiary bombs dropped on Middlesbrough. One high explosive caused considerable damage to 150 houses in the Glebe Road, St. Paul's area of the town. Twenty-one people were injured and one was killed.

Four of the bombs fell at the corner of Linthorpe Road and Park Road South, causing damage to the Park Hotel. Two others dropped on Ayresome Ironworks and caused sufficient damage to ensure that 'pig-iron production would be stopped for six to eight weeks'.

Numerous incendiaries were dropped but most landed in Linthorpe cemetery and did little damage.

On the same night, five high explosives fell near Ladgates Farm, Brotton, and two other bombs fell behind Sun Street, Thornaby: neither of these attacks caused casualties.

Ladgates Farm, situated off the Saltburn—Brotton road had a narrow escape during a bombing raid in the early hours of 12 May 1941, as this aerial photograph shows. Three craters —possibly four—can be seen very close to the farm buildings. A fourth crater, clearly caused by a larger calibre bomb, was wider of the mark. [Photo. *Author's collection*]

June, 1941. In the summer of 1941, Tom Sawyer (left) was a Squadron Leader flying Halifax bombers with No.76 Squadron, based at Middleton-St-George, now Teesside airport.

He and his six-man crew had a narrow escape from disaster in the skies over Middlesbrough on 20 June, 1941, when they found themselves flying *through* the town's balloon barrage.

' *I took my first Halifax Mk1 on an operation on the night of 20 June, 1941. Kiel was the target, but I nearly didn't get there because it almost ended before it had begun. Middleton-St-George was situated about ten miles from the centre of Middlesbrough, and this industrial town and port was protected against enemy attack with balloons, besides the normal AA guns and searchlights*

'*Having taken off at dusk on a clear summer evening, we made a wide circle inland before I set the course given to me by our navigator. Concentrating intently on the instruments and cockpit adjustments with my head down in the 'office' to make sure that everything was in order, I had just lined up the compass to the correct heading when Butch Heaton at the wireless set suddenly called over the intercom: "We're heading into the balloon barrage, Skipper" - and at almost the same time I heard in my earphones the alarming high-pitched buzz of the 'squeakers' which indicated that we were indeed flying close to the balloons.*

'*This warning device was broadcast from the ground where the balloons were being flown, on the same frequency as our R/T, and supposedly to warn us that we were approaching a balloon defended area. The range was very limited for obvious reasons, and in this case was so short that we were in amongst the balloons before we picked up the warning.*

'*We were then flying at 4,000 feet, and glancing upwards I saw those damn great fat balloons sitting there about 7—800 feet above us, and clearly visible in the setting sun, although the ground below was in dark shadow. I couldn't see the cables of, course, but the balloons themselves indicated the direction of the wind since they all naturally pointed on the same heading, and I edged gingerly to one side to fly exactly between two balloons ahead of us in that particular line. They were fairly wide apart and there was room enough but it felt rather a tight squeeze at the time. Then, following the direction they were all pointing, I eased between the next two, and then the next, with my eyes glued upwards and climbing as steeply as I dared to try and get above the brutes, and finally breaking clear almost level with the last one, giving a cheerful 'All Clear' to the rest of my crew who had been suffering in silence while I had been juggling cautiously to get out of it. I realised that I was soaked with sweat as we settled down on course and began to relax, although there had been no physical exertion at all...The rest of the trip was a piece of cake by comparison...*'
Group Capt Tom Sawyer, DFC: *Only Owls and Bloody Fools Fly at Night,* (William Kimber, 1982)

Halifax Mk.1 bombing-up at a northern aerodrome.
[Photo. *courtesy of the Northern Echo*]

June, 1941. On 19 June 1941, King George VI and Queen Elizabeth made a surprise visit to Middlesbrough. As soon as their Majesties' visit became known, thousands of people flocked to vantage points and gave the royal couple a great welcome.

They were greeted by large crowds when they arrived at Albert park to inspect members of the local civil defence services before going on to visit Thornaby aerodrome.

During their short stay in the town, the King and Queen were escorted by the Mayor and Mayoress of Middlesbrough, Cllr Sir William Crosthwaite and Lady Crosthwaite.

[Photo. *Author's collection*]

THEY'RE USING **Osram** LAMPS ON BOARD

Your favourite lamps are helping to bring Victory

The Battle of the Atlantic is being lost!

The reasons why:

1. German U-boats, German bombers and the German fleet sink and seriously damage between them every month a total of 700 000 to 1 million tons of British and allied shipping.

2. All attempts at finding a satisfactory means of defence against the German U-boats or the German bombers have failed disastrously.

3. Even President Roosevelt has openly stated that for every five ships sunk by Germany, Britain and America between them can only build two new ones. All attempts to launch a larger shipbuilding programme in America have failed.

4. Britain is no longer in a position to secure her avenues of supply. The population of Britain has to do with about half the ration that the population of Germany gets. Britain, herself, can only support 40 % of her population from her own resources in spite of the attempts made to increase the amount of land under cultivation. If the war is continued until 1942, 60 % of the population of Britain will starve!

All this means that starvation in Britain is not to be staved off. At the most it can be postponed, but whether starvation comes this year or at the beginning of next doesn't make a ha'porth of difference. Britain must starve because she is being cut off from her supplies.

Britain's losing the Battle of the Atlantic means

Britain's losing the war!

July, 1941. Not everything that was dropped by the Luftwaffe had physical destruction as its goal. This propaganda leaflet (left) was part of a prolonged attempt to undermine the morale of inhabitants of these islands. Like similar efforts by the British over Germany, the policy of persuasion had little or no effect. This particular example dropped on Danby moors, North Yorkshire, on 18 July 1941. [Photo. *A.Askew*]

The photograph (left) shows the Royal Naval frigate HMS *Rother*, launched at Smith's Dock on 20 November 1941, undergoing sea trials off the Tees in 1942. The vessel survived the war and was scrapped at Troon in April 1955.

The photograph (below) shows the partly submerged minesweeper HMS *Halcyon*, which was mined off the Tees and towed into Smith's Dock for repair. The date of the photograph is unknown.
[Photos. *Cleveland County Libraries*]

1942. Teesside's role as a major centre for ship-building and ship repairs has long since faded, but in earlier times the situation was far different.

During the Second World War the Tees' yards of Furness Shipbuilding (at Haverton Hill) and the Smith's Dock Company (at South Bank), together with William Gray's yard at Hartlepool were thrown into a fervour of activity and produced large numbers of naval vessels, including frigates and landing barges.

The crew of Do.217 U5+HS of 8./KG2. **L-R:** *Feldwebel* Joachim Lehnis (pilot), *Unteroffizier* Hans Maneke (wireless operator), *Leutnant* Rudolf Matern (observer), and *Oberfeldwebel* Heinrich Richter (gunner/mechanic). [Photo. *Kurt Matern*]

January, 1942.   In the early evening of 15 January 1942, Holland-based aircraft of Luftwaffe bomber unit *Kampfgeschwader 2* launched attacks against shipping and port installations along England's east coast. Among those taking part was a Dornier 217E-4 of 8./KG2, coded U5+HS. It was piloted by *Feldwebel* Joachim Lehnis, who had been ordered to attack a convoy that was 'eastwards of Middlesbrough'. There is a possibility that Lehnis dropped two bombs on Skinningrove Ironworks at about 17.30 hours and one bomb on Eston Jetty at about 17.55 hours before dive-bombing the steamship *Empire Bay* (2,824 GRT) that was anchored one mile off Hartlepool and waiting to join a southbound convoy that was steaming down from the north. The bomber straddled the ship with five or six bombs, causing structural damage that eventually caused the vessel to sink.

The Dornier reportedly suffered engine damage from gunfire during the engagement with the ship before flying inland towards the Tees barrage balloon cordon. The bomber, which was by then trailing black smoke and losing height, subsequently collided with the anchor cable of a balloon flying 4,000 feet above the North Tees' jetties.

The Dornier lost a substantial part of its starboard wing in the collision and crashed on to the private railway sidings of the Dorman, Long steelworks, close by what is now the South Bank railway station. There were no survivors. Three badly charred bodies - believed at the time to be those of Lehnis, Matern and Richter (see photo) - were recovered and later buried at the Acklam Road cemetery, Thornaby. The fourth man, believed at the time to be Hans Maneke, was not found. Because the siding were required for urgent war work, most of the wreckage was buried in the crater and the track re-laid.

The wreckage was 're-discovered on 26 November 1997 by Water Board workers laying sewers for an intended business park development. Following the discovery, excavation of the site was undertaken by a team of Royal Engineers working with specialists from No. 5131 Bomb Disposal

Squadron, RAF. The mortal remains of the fourth member of the crew were subsequently unearthed deep in the excavation. Forensic examination showed them to be those of Heinrich Richter and pointed to a confusion of identities when the other corpses were buried in 1942. Richter was buried alongside his comrades on 14 October 1998 during a ceremony attended by the German Consul-General to Britain, the German Air Attaché, three local mayors, the representatives of twenty-two ex-Servicemen's associations and some 200 members of the general public.

Heinrich Richter, gunner/mechanic of Do.217 U5+HS (8./KG2) was one of three brothers. All served in the German Armed Forces and none survived the war. [Photo. *Werner Feige*]

The burial of Heinrich Richter at Acklam Road Cemetery, Thornaby, 14 October 1998.
[Photo. *Stuart McMillan*]

Their demand for water outstripped hydrant supplies, which had to be supplemented by pumping additional sources from the swimming baths (located at the point from where this picture was taken) and from the river Tees, almost a mile away.

Initially, the cause of the blaze was considered to have been accidental. However, in June of the same year, Dickson & Benson's department store in Dundas Street, and 'Cheap' Wilson's in Corporation Road, suffered similar fates; later in the same month, Upton's, at Garnet Street corner, was also set on fire.

There was growing scepticism that the outbreaks were, in fact, accidental, but it was not until a young schoolboy was discovered pushing burning paper through the letterbox of another store that the cause was finally ascertained.
{Photo. *E. Baxter/Evening Gazette*}

28 March 1942. The fire-scarred shell of Binns department store stands roofless and floorless at the corner of Linthorpe Road and Newport Road (this view taken from the rear in Gilkes Street).

The blaze, which had raged for six hours the previous evening and which had been watched by large crowds, required the efforts of 350 firemen and forty-eight appliances to bring it under control.

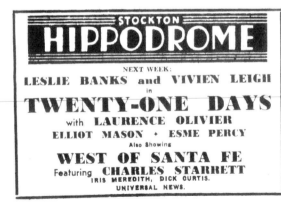

April, 1942. Workmen repairing damage to the 24-inch cast iron gas main and the sewer in Laws Street, Newport after an air raid on the night of 15-16 April. 1942. [Photo. *J. Todd*]

Enemy bombers attacked at 11.46pm on 15 April, 1942, and four high explosives fell in a line across Carlow Street, Mills Street, Laws Street and Newport recreation ground; four bombs also fell in the river. The first stick of bombs caused major casualties: twenty-eight people killed and thirty-nine injured. Damage to property was widespread. Thirty-nine houses were rendered uninhabitable, a further 1,707 were less seriously affected and 1,156 people were made homeless.

Bombs fell elsewhere in the area on the same night. Seven high explosives and two that failed to explode were dropped on Saltburn. One bomb exploded between an empty air raid shelter in Station Street and housing in Exeter Street. The shelter was destroyed and four properties required demolition. One person was killed and eleven were injured.

In the Marske area, four high explosives produced only minor damage. Seven high explosives and one unexploded bomb fell around New Marske and four of the former caused severe destruction at Sparrow Farm.

Further afield, two bombs fell in the Guisborough area but caused no damage; ten dropped in open areas in the Barnes Farm/Warren Wood/Mutton Scalp Lane area of Skelton; eight high explosives fell in open country around Loftus; and ten fell in open areas around Redcar.

Given the number of bombs that fell on the area that night, the casualties were mercifully light . Clearly, the German bomb aimers were off target—particularly in view of the fact that they were supposed to be bombing Sunderland.

Defend Your Own Town!

JOIN THE HOME GUARD A-A UNIT

● **Suitable for all men aged 18-65.**

● **Training is not strenuous and is only three nights per week.**

● **When trained—and training is only for a limited period—only one night in eight. Sleeping quarters and food provided.**

● **Arrangements have been made for shift workers to receive training during the day-time.**

● **Travelling expenses allowed.**

● **Hundreds required URGENTLY to release regular trained men for more active duties.**

DO YOUR BIT!

Why not ask for particulars? There is no obligation. For this purpose a BUREAU HAS BEEN OPENED AT UPTONS' SERVICE DEPOT (adjoining the Gaumont Palace), 208-210, LINTHORPE ROAD, MIDDLES-BROUGH, through the courtesy of Messrs. Uptons, Ltd. This will be open TO-MORROW (Saturday), 2 to 5 p.m. & SUNDAY, 10 to 12 a.m. and 3 to 5 p.m.

Opposite page. There were at least two anti-aircraft gun sites on Teesside that were equipped with the Z Rocket Projector. They were at Brambles Farm and at Portrack Lane, near the Tees Bridge.. They were in action for the first time in April, 1942. It is believed that they were manned by Home Guard personnel from July 1942.

The Z gun, also known as the UP (unrotated projectile) weapon, had been introduced for high altitude defence. It fired fin-stabilised 3-inch diameter rockets that were 6ft 4inches long, weighed 56lbs (including a warhead of 22lbs) and were fused to explode at a pre-set time after launch. Each rocket battery contained 64 twin projectors that fired a salvo of 128 rockets simultaneously. The missiles accelerated to 1,000mph in 1½seconds before coasting to the altitude at which they were set to explode. Their maximum altitude was 19,000 feet. The device used the 'scatter-gun' technique and was highly inaccurate. It was, however, psychologically impressive to both friend and foe alike!

When the battery engaged raiders, multitudes of rockets were launched into the sky with a terrific rushing noise ('like an express train') before exploding in one thunderous, reverberating roar that shook the area below: a lethal giant firework that bracketed a large expanse of sky with the brilliant red of detonating shells and unseen shards of potentially withering shrapnel. It seems that the Z gun was never a successful destroyer of aircraft but it did put the wind up at least some Luftwaffe crews. *Oberleutnant* Werner Borner, of 4./KG2, who raided Middlesbrough on the night of 7-8 July 1942, had this to say:

'Today, we were sent yet again on the long trip which is also one of the most unpleasant, ie. to Middlesbrough In this area they have a bright fireworks' spectacular during each air raid and no crew has yet ascertained whether it is bluff or whether the sky really is on fire and full of iron when you fly through it. We only know that the 'mortar man', as I call it, rises 700m into the air as a small fireball and then breaks into hundreds of small bright shining projectiles which spread over a 45° sector, rise to 3,000m and there fizzle out. If you get among that lot you are beyond help—it's sharp ammunition you're talking about.'

The Z Rocket Projector...and its scatter-gun technique.
[Photo. *Author's collection*]

In 1942, the Great Ayton firemen were issued with new uniforms and they used that opportunity to pose for a group photograph—in a most unusual setting! **Front row** (L—R): unknown, Billy Teasdale, Fred Gibson. **Middle row**: Maurice Heavisides, George Smith, Walter Fletcher, Ernie Burdon. **Back row**: Kit Johnson, unknown, Billy Haigh. .[Photo. *M. Heavisides*]

Beat 'FIREBOMB FRITZ'

BRITAIN SHALL NOT BURN

BRITAIN'S FIRE GUARD IS BRITAIN'S DEFENCE

shelter from which appointed personnel (known as 'firewatchers') would keep watch during air raid attacks—especially at night—for outbreaks caused by falling incendiary bombs.
[Photo. Middlesbrough *Evening Gazette*]

September 1939. Camouflaged petrol storage tanks (below) at ICI's riverside site. These storage facilities were hit during the night of 7-8 July 1942.
[Photo. *courtesy of ICI*]

8 July 1942. Middlesbrough's balloon barrage flies high over the town while petrol storage tanks at ICI Billingham continue to burn following the previous night's attack on the plant by German bombers of *Kampfgeschwader 2* (KG2)

Wright's Tower House department store stands out white against the pall of smoke that snakes its way over the tall chimneys of the Ironmasters' District. The office building of the Constantine Shipping Company (foreground) in Borough Road is surmounted by a small brick

July, 1942. In the early hours of Sunday, 26 July 1942, twenty--two Dornier 217 bombers of *Kampfgeschwader 2* (KG2) attacked Middlesbrough with high explosives, oil bombs and hundreds of incendiary bombs. It was the town's most destructive air raid.

The bombers' target markers suggest that ICI Billingham and the Ironmasters' District were the intended targets, but, as on previous occasions, the area south of the railway seems to have taken the brunt of the attack.

The principal zones affected were the Wilson Street—Station Street area (mainly high explosives), the neighbourhood that embraces Clifton Street—Linthorpe Road—Waterloo Road (mainly high explosives). Less badly affected were the LNER Goods' Station-Francis Street area, north of the railway line (high explosives and incendiariy bombs), and also the locality where Newport Road meets Corporation Road (mainly incendiary bombs).

This was the night that the Leeds' Hotel took a direct hit and the Co-op Victoria Hall, Linthorpe Road was burned to the ground.

26 July 1942. The ruins of the Leeds' Hotel, at the junction of Linthorpe Road and Wilson Street, Middlesbrough, after an air raid in the early hours of the morning. [Photo. Middlesbrough *Evening Gazette*]

In the evening of the same day, the German News Service in Berlin claimed that the bombers had scored ' numerous hits on iron works and harbour works and heavy explosions broke out in the target area.' In fact, only two industrial premises south of the Tees—Dorman, Long Britannia Works and Acklam Ironworks suffered notifiable damage. Damage of another kind was far greater: sixteen people were killed and fifty were injured; sixty-eight houses and seventy-six business premises were rendered uninhabitable and some 200 people were made homeless. In addition, some 1,000 houses and 220 business premises sustained minor damage.

Opposite. Eight of the nine LNER employees who received commendations for 'brave conduct in civil defence' at Middlesbrough Goods' Yard during the night of 25-26 July 1942. The ninth person was J. McClusky. The men worked through the raid, unhitching and moving burning wagons in order to stop fires spreading .

Back (L—R): R.W. Kitching (Yard Inspector), A. Bradshaw, J. Charlesworth. **Front** (L—R): J. H. Jackson, A.E. Grace, J. Binks, N. G. Reid.

Arthur Bradshaw was awarded the British Empire Medal for 'gallant conduct and good service' during the attack.
[Photo. *via Pat Harbron,*]

Bomb-damaged properties in Wilson Street, Middlesbrough, some days after the raid of 25-26 July 1942. This photograph was taken from the bottom of Albert Road and looks west towards the bottom of Linthorpe Road. The building on the left is the Wellington Hotel. The A66 road now runs where the buildings on the right stood in 1942.[Photo. *Author's collection*]

July, 1942. Middlesbrough Corporation bus-driver Ron Nelson and his conductor, Tommy James, pose for the camera while resting at the Levick Crescent terminus before commencing their run to the 'Transporter via Linthorpe Road'. Of particular interest are the white-painted mudguards, the partly masked windows and the almost totally masked sidelights—all sure indicators that this photograph was taken in wartime. [Photo. *Ron Nelson*]

Because of the Blackout Regulations, road vehicles were permitted only minimum lighting during the hours of darkness: sidelights were allowed to emit only the merest pinpricks of light, while headlights were heavily masked to ensure that only a feeble beam shone on the near-side kerb almost immediately in front of the bus. Bus interiors were subject to similar controls: blue bulbs were used to produce the minimum of illumination and the upper halves of windows were stained a similar colour to reduce the amount of light detectable from the air.

Driving was very difficult in such circumstances and at the end of their shifts, crews often felt as if their 'eyes were on six-inch stalks'. The situation was worse in a fog or during those times when the town's smoke defences were being used in anticipation of an air raid. On those occasions, the conductor would sometimes perch on the front near-side mudguard and call steering directions to the driver through the cab's side window.

If a raid did occur during a journey, the bus would stop at the nearest shelter so that passengers could take cover. If the crew intended to follow suit, the driver would remove the steering wheel and take it with him. That was particularly the case in the early days of the war, when the threat of invasion was very real and there was the possibility that invading Germans might steal the vehicle!

Because of the system of split shifts, bus crews might start work at 6.00am and not finish until 11.00pm— a long day by any standards! In 1942, a driver's pay for a sixty-hour week was £5.17.3d gross (£5.86 in today's currency) and £4.12.6d (£4.625) after tax.

Home Guard and Civil Defence exercise in Guisborough, July 1942 [Photo. *courtesy of the Northern Echo*]

July, 1942. (opposite). One of a number of Spitfires purchased from subscriptions donated by the people of Middlesbrough during the war is made ready to join its squadron.

Schemes to raise funds to finance the war effort were constantly being initiated by the government and by local communities. Perhaps one of the first to be initiated locally was in 1940, when the then chairman of Middlesbrough Motor Club, Bill Oliver, proposed a scheme to provide The Royal Air Force with a Spitfire that would bear the town's name and coat of arms. The estimated cost was £5,000

.The club agreed to sponsor a 'Spitfire Week' and the Mayor, Cllr Sir William Crosthwaite, lent his support to the venture by inviting the public to subscribe to the fund. Club members organised house-to-house collections, while other money-making schemes (including a concert in the *Odeon* cinema and a series of dances at the *Grand Hotel)* provided additional contributions. The target was soon exceeded.

THE PLAZA, Stockton   5.45—CONTINUOUS—10.30.
MONDAY NEXT.

FOR THREE DAYS ONLY.

Old Mother Riley in Paris

Also Don Terry and Rosalind Keith in A FIGHT TO THE FINISH.
Thursday.—THERE AIN'T NO JUSTICE.

Below. October 1942. Canadian Sergeant F.E. Jones, RCAF, of No.249 Squadron at the controls of a Spitfire purchased by the citizens of Darlington. [Photo. *IWM Neg.CH3977*]

On 20 November, during the course of a light supper organised by the motor club, Bill Oliver presented the Mayor with a cheque for £5,700, made payable to the Ministry of Aircraft Production. The town's first Spitfire (serial R7122) was purchased early in 1941. On 1 June of the year it was issued to the newly -formed 123 Squadron, RAF, based at Turnhouse (now Edinburgh airport). The squadron became operational on 8 June and was initially engaged on shipping patrols off the Scottish coast. On 9 July 1941, the aircraft was engaged in aerial combat and was damaged beyond repair. It had been in service for just five weeks.

One of a number of Spitfires 'purchased' by the citizens of Middlesbrough. [Photo. *AW Zealand*]

3 August, 1942. Bank Holiday Monday, 3 August 1942, shortly after a low-flying Dornier 217 bomber had aimed four 500kg bombs at Middlesbrough railway station.

Two of the bombs scored direct hits and caused much damage to the station canopy but only slight damage to the railway lines. The third bomb struck Kirkup's warehouse in Station Street, demolishing it and the adjacent tailor's shop in which Peter Niman and William Thornelowe were working: both were killed. The fourth destroyed properties in Crown Street.

Freight traffic was moving through the station again within twenty-four hours of the attack and passenger traffic some eight hours after that. Sadly, eight people were killed and fifty eight were injured.

A memorial plaque to those who lost their lives was unveiled on the station's main concourse on 3 August 1998.

[Photo. *Author's collection*]

Top left. Middlesbrough station before that attack. [Photo.*Author's collection*]

Above. The North platform, struck by the first bomb. [Photo..*Author's collection*]

Left. An artist's impression of the raid by Stuart McMillan.
[Photo. *Stuart McMillan*]

SAVE YOUR BONES

Do **YOU** know
what is made from them?

1 TON OF SALVAGED BONES WILL PRODUCE

2 Cwts. of GREASE *which will provide*
NITRO-GLYCERINE *for* **SHELLS,**
LUBRICATING OIL *for* **GUNS** and **TANKS,**
SOAP, MEDICINAL PRODUCTS.

AND

3-CWTS. of GLUE *used in the manufacture of*
AIRCRAFT, TANKS, GUNS, SHELLS, SHIPS
CAMOUFLAGE, A.R.P *and other War purposes*

AND

1-Cwt. of FEEDING MEAT and BONE
MEAL *providing the protein concentrate for*
450 PIGS *or* **8,960 HENS** *for* **1 DAY**

AND

9-Cwt. of BONE FERTILISER *sufficient to provide*
the phosphates for **42** *acres of Land yielding*
36 Tons of Potatoes *or Wheat to make* **4,500 Loaves.**
(The 5-Cwts. Balance is moisture).

Every bit of the bone can be used, if **YOU** save it.

P D 106886/H.O./100M

Above. 7 August 1942. Middlesbrough school children undergo gas drill in the Russell Street area during an ARP exercise. One of the principal points to emerge from the practice was that many of the town's citizens had ceased to carry their masks. They paid the penalty when they were caught by clouds of practice gas that were released in congested parts of the town. Several hundred people were queuing outside the *Odeon* cinema, in Corporation Road, when a cloud was released near there. At least two-thirds of them did not have their respirators. A number dashed for safety, but others had to suffer acute discomfort for several minutes after being caught in the cloud and inhaling its contents. Their comments about the ARP were not recorded! [Photo. *E. Baxter/Evening Gazette*]

Gunner Robert Watmore.
[Photo. *via John Porteus*]

September,1942. In September 1942, Whitby's Metropole Hotel was being used as a motor-vehicle driver training centre by the 52nd A.A. Training Regiment, Royal Artillery.

Trainees and Staff were billeted in the hotel and the training vehicles were kept in the car park at the back of the building. On the night of 6 September, 1942, trainee soldier Robert Watmore was on guard in the car park, seemingly having exchanged that duty for a similar one at Sandsend.

14-year old John Porteus, who lived nearby, used to take a nightly cup of tea to whoever was on guard duty. 6 September was no exception and at 11.30pm he took one to Watmore. The air raid siren had sounded earlier that night and enemy aircraft had been heard in the vicinity, but all was quiet when John handed over the tea to the 19-year old soldier.

Planes were overhead again when John made his way home. Shortly afterwards, perhaps the only bomb to drop on Whitby that night landed in the car park, where its explosive force destroyed some thirty vehicles and killed Robert Watmore.

John Porteus claims that the soldier was the only member of the British armed forces to die as a result of enemy action at Whitby, where thousands of forces' personnel were trained.

John, who now lives in Station Road, Whitby, never forgot the young gunner from Newbridge, Edinburgh, and it always bothered him that the incident had not been publicly recorded. In 1992, he decided to do something about it.

On Sunday, 6 September 1992, a bronze commemorative plaque provided by John was unveiled in front of Welton Court flats by the town's Mayor, Cllr Wastell. It is near the spot where Gunner Watmore died .

1996. John Porteus alongside the plaque. The Metropole Hotel is behind.
[Photos. *Author*]

Close by
During an air raid
on the night of 6th September 1942
GUNNER ROBERT WATMORE
aged 19 years
from Newbridge Nr. Edinburgh,
serving with the 52nd A.A. Training
Regiment, Royal Artillery,
became the only British Soldier
to be killed in Whitby by Enemy
Action in the Second World War.

Lest we forget.

September, 1942. Two Messerschmitt 210A-1 aircraft of the sixteenth *Staffel* of *Kampfgeschwader 6* (16./KG6) were shot down over Cleveland on the morning of 6 September 1942.

The German aircraft were on an armed reconnaissance mission and had been detected by radar while they were still way out over the North Sea. Twenty minutes before the raiders reached the English coast, two Typhoon fighters of No.1 Squadron were scrambled from Acklington, Northumberland, with orders to intercept. The fighters spotted their targets seaward of Redcar and at an altitude of 28,500 feet. They engaged them over Lackenby, where the 210's jettisoned bombs after realising that they were being pursued.

One of the German aircraft (coded 2H+CA) crashed alongside the reservoir close by Fell Briggs Farm, New Marske. The other (coded 2H+HA) was chased as far as Robin Hood's Bay before being shot down: it crashed at Fylingthorpe.

The two-man crew of the second raider managed to bale out and they survived the encounter unscathed but the crew of 2H+CA were killed: they were buried in Acklam Road Cemetery, Thornaby, were they still lie.

Upper right. Me210A-1 (2H+CA) at New Marske.
Near right. Hawker Typhoons.
Far right. Me. 210's
[All photos. *Author's collection*]

1943. Women were given the option of entering one of the women's branches of the armed forces or of taking 'direct' employment (which would release men for active service). Mrs J. Turner of Stockton (front row, 3rd from right) chose the latter. She was employed as a furnace-worker at Dorman, Long's Bowesfield Lane Works, where as one of a team of four women, she preheated iron sheets prior to their being corrugated for use in the production of Anderson air-raid shelters. The women—whose work was always arduous but which, apparently, eased as experience taught more effective techniques of handling—worked a three-shift system and a six-day week for a weekly wage of £2.0s. 0d. (£2.00 in decimal currency).

[Photo. *Mrs J. Turner*]

April, 1943. On 22 October 1987, the Middlesbrough *Evening Gazette* carried a brief report that paid tribute to a town's wartime generosity—and shed an illuminating sidelight on how values and priorities are susceptible to the passing of time. The report concerned the 'Thornaby' Stirling bomber.

By April 1943 the war effort was costing Britain £11 million a day. One way of helping to meet such expenditure was by organising both national and local War Savings Weeks, usually based on a particular theme and with a specific end in view. The idea of giving would-be subscribers such a point of focus was probably pioneered by the 'Spitfire Funds' that were introduced so successfully in the latter half of 1940.

These aimed to encourage communities throughout the country to subscribe enough money to purchase 'their own' Spitfire. Each aircraft bought would bear the name of the community responsible for its acquisition.

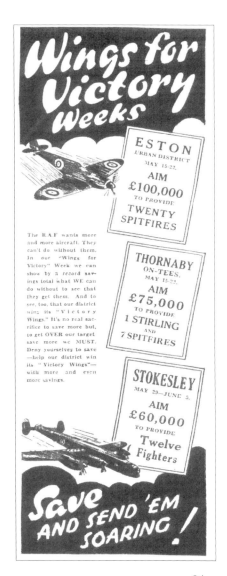

In 1943, Thornaby-on-Tees organised a 'Wings for Victory' fund-raising campaign for the week of 15-22 May. The town set itself the target of £75,000, enough to buy seven Spitfires and one heavy bomber. Such was the town's generosity that when the fund closed the target had been exceeded by £25,920. The bomber 'purchased' by Thornaby was a Mark III Short Stirling (serial number EH875) that had been delivered to No.15 Squadron, Milldenhall on 6 May, some weeks after the fund-raising had got underway but nine days before the start of Wings' Week, which was to be the climax of the effort. The aircraft was allocated the squadron code LS-S(*Sugar*) and began operational service on 21 May 1943, when it successfully completed a mine-laying operation off the Frisian Islands. Following that, S(*Sugar*) carried out a further twenty-two operations—including an attack on Cologne on 28 June, when German flak was sufficiently close to shatter the pilot's windscreen—before it took part in the first large-scale attack on Berlin on the night of 23-24 August 1943.

For eighteen of the operations prior to Berlin, the aircraft had been piloted by Sergeant E.R. Cornell. When it lifted off from Mildenhall at 8.37pm en-route to the German capital, Cornell (newly promoted to Pilot Officer) was again at the controls. The usual members of his crew were with him: Sergeant N.P. Collins (navigator), Flight Sergeant E. Gorbert (wireless operator), Sergeant W. S. Frame (bomb aimer), Sergeant H. Bottomley (air gunner), Sergeant J.C. Thompson (air gunner) and Sergeant F.T. Morris (flight engineer).

As was to be expected, the raid proved to be very difficult. The 700-plus bombers (including 124 Stirlings) that took part met particularly fierce resistance as they approached the target area. Heavy concentrations of flak layered the sky with shrapnel to an altitude of 12,000 feet.

Above that there roamed an estimated 150 German night fighters, whose stalking game was aided by 200 searchlights that created ' a wall of light' that robbed the night of its protective darkness. Sergeant Ferris Newton, a flight engineer in a Halifax of No.76 Squadron, Holme-on-Spalding Moor, described the scene:

'The first thing we have to do is to fly through a wall of searchlights: there are hundreds of them—in cones and in clusters. It's a wall of light with very few breaks and behind that wall is an even fiercer light, glowing red and green and blue. It is pretty obvious that it is going to be hell over the target. There is only one comfort, and it has been a comfort to me all the time that we have been going over, and that is that it is quite soundless; the row of the engines drowns everything else. It is like running straight into the most gigantic display of fireworks in the world.'
[**quoted by Martin Middlesbrook in** *The Berlin Raids,* **Viking, 1988**]

Bomber Command lost fifty-six (7.9%) aircraft, thirty-one of them falling to the north of the city along a corridor some sixty-five miles long. Of the 124 Stirlings that took part, sixteen failed to return: S-*Sugar* was one of them. The 'Thornaby' Stirling crashed some three kilometres from Schönwalde: there were no survivors.

On 22 October 1987, the Middlesbrough *Evening Gazette* reported that the Aero Centre Museum (which was then located on the site of the old Thornaby aerodrome) had acquired the log-book of S-*Sugar* and the Air Ministry plaque that recognised Thornaby's achievement in raising sufficient funds to 'purchase' the aircraft. Both had been presented to the town forty-three years earlier and both had, one assumes, rested on council property since then.

That they should finally be donated to a museum dedicated to keeping alive the memory of the town's aviation past would seem to be appropriate—but the fact that both items had been retrieved from a rubbish skip located at the council offices is surely a sad indication of the lack of regard we sometimes have for the sacrifices that others made on our behalf.

[**NOTE:** Of the 125,000 aircrew who served with the squadrons and training units of RAF Bomber Command during 1939-45, nearly 50% were killed. It was the highest loss rate sustained by any arm of the British armed forces during the Second World War]

22 October 1987. Doug Cameron, partner in the Thornaby Aero Centre Museum, shows off the Air Ministry plaque and the log-book of the 'Thornaby' Stirling bomber. [Middlesbrough *Evening Gazette*]

When the war broke out, Olive Coulson was already well-established in local operatic circles. She was a member of Stockton's (then well known) Brunswick Church Choir, she was a winner of a number of northern eisteddfods, and occasional singer on BBC radio. In September, 1939, her career took on a new dimension , that of troop entertainer, when she was asked to sing at a troop concert at the town's YMCA, which was sited in the Temperance Hall. It was the first of some 700 such concerts she was to give during the course of the war.

At about the same time, she was invited to join a local Concert Party (*The Searchlights*) that was being formed to entertain troops of Northern Command as part of the Voluntary Entertainment Service (VES). *The Searchlights,* formed by Billy Scarrow, who ran a pierrot show on Redcar beach before the war, had a number of well-known local artistes, including Harry Whitcomb (comedian), Pat Fox (baritone) and Billy Burdon, another Redcar beach entertainer, who did a double act with Scarrow that had " the soldiers really howling with laughter".

Olive used to sing solo, as well as in duet with Harold Peacock (when they were billed as *The Aristocrats*). Initially, the party travelled in two buses—one for the orchestra that accompanied the artistes—until transport difficulties caused the orchestra to be dropped.

In addition, Olive continued her voluntary work for the Stockton YMCA and visited all of the local gun-sites with other entertainers. Usually they performed in front of a full house, but many were the times that the alarm bell warned of incoming raiders and Olive found herself singing to only a couple of soldiers who were off duty.

When the war was over, she sang at a number of Welcome Home concerts, but one occasion in particular stands high in memory: 'the wonderful "Thank You" concert for Northern Command artistes that was held in Saltburn Spa on 15 August 1945'. All of the performers who had helped out during the war did a spot on the show and in a hall that was full to capacity. Among the songs featured by *The Aristocrats* were: *With a song in my heart, Smoke gets in your eyes, At the Balalaika,* and *I'll see you again.*

Olive readily admits that she enjoyed the war "singing wise", but the reality of the conflict had never been far away. She remembers attending a concert at the Bailey Street Schools in Stockton for troops (" I thought that they were only kids") destined to go over seas the next day. "We had a fantastic night, just singing together...A long time afterwards, I learned that they had all been killed going out. Somehow, you don't forget."

1945. Olive Coulson proudly wears her VES Northern Command badge and her YMCA North East War Worker badge.
[Photo. *Olive Coulson*]

1988. Olive Coulson with a 1945 concert poster that places her at the top of the bill. [Photo. *courtesy of the Whitby Gazette*]

THE MISSIONS TO SEAMEN
MIDDLESBROUGH

GRAND
VARIETY CONCERT
(arranged by Jack Mendelson)

BY ARTISTES OF THE
NORTHERN COMMAND

TUESDAY, 30th MARCH, 1943

commencing 7-30 p.m.

PROGRAMME

MABEL THORMAN	Piano Solo
DOROTHY SMURTHWAITE	Popular Songstress
JACK MENDELSON	Cartoonist
MOLLY HILTON	Zylophonist and Speciality Dancer
FRED HAY	Yodeller
PAT SYMINGTON	Vocalist and Dancer
ERNIE O'BRIEN	Comedian
OLIVE COULSON	B.B.C. Contralto, Gold Medallist
FRED PROBEE	Mimic
At the Piano	MABEL THORMAN
Compere :	T. HILTON

1944. During the war years , the tug boats of the Tees-Towing Company were rarely idle for any length of time. In addition to the services required by commercial shipping, the crews of those 'work-horses' of the river were also kept busy with salvage works arising from enemy action as well as dealing with ships of the Royal Navy and those of Allies, which were regular visitors to the port.

Such vessels ranged from large destroyers to landing-craft, the latter increasingly in evidence during 1943-44 as the build-up to the Normandy landings gained momentum. Perhaps the strangest tow the tugs had to provide during those years was for two concrete caissons (code-named '*Phoenix*') that formed part of the Mulberry Harbour used to aid the D-Day landings

The photograph shows the first of the caissons, built at William Gray's Drydock, Graythorpe, in 1944, being manoeuvered out of the drydock prior to being towed to the southern assembly point by Royal Navy tugs.. [Photo. *W. Haigh Parry*]

Mynarski backed his way down the fuselage to the exit. There he drew himself to attention, saluted Brophy and then baled out. Shortly afterwards, the Lancaster hit the ground at a shallow angle close to the French village of Gaudiempré, near Amiens. By a twist of fate, Brophy survived the crash and spent the rest of the war as a POW. After his release, he was able to tell of Mynarski's bravery.

Andrew Mynarski did not survive for his clothing was already aflame when he baled out of the Lancaster. Frenchmen watched his fiery descent and though he was alive when they reached him, he was far beyond help and died from severe burns shortly afterwards. His body now lies in the cemetery at Meharicourt, France.

When Brophy was able to tell his story, Andrew Mynarski was awarded a posthumous Victoria Cross. It was gazetted on 11 October, 1946.

June, 1944. On the night 12-13 June, 1944, Lancaster bombers of No.419 (Moose)Squadron, RCAF, took off from Middleton-St-George (now Teesside airport) to attack the marshalling yards at Cambrai, France. Pilot Officer Andrew Mynarski was the mid-upper gunner of the Lancaster coded VR-A. Shortly after crossing the French coast, the bomber was severely damaged and set on fire by a German night fighter and the pilot gave the order to bale out.

Mynarski was preparing to jump from the rear exit when he saw that his friend Pat Brophy, the rear gunner, was trapped in his rear turret. With the aircraft in flames, Mynarski ignored his own safety and made desperate efforts to rescue his friend. It was futile. Brophy was the first to recognise the fact and finally managed to persuade Mynarski to go. By then, Mynarski's clothing was burning but he left only with reluctance.

With his clothing aflame and his gaze fixed on his friend,

Upper left. Canadian Lancaster bombers at Middleton-St-George (now Teesside airport), March 1945. [Photo. *via Chris Sheehan*]

Right. Pilot Officer Andrew Mynarski, VC.
[Photo.*Canada DND/PL38261*]

March, 1945. Croft aerodrome, 11.35am on 22 March, 1945. A Lancaster bomber (coded WL-F) of No.434(Bluenose)Squaron, Royal Canadian Air Force, disappears in a cloud of explosive fire and smoke. Half an hour earlier, the aircraft had crashed and burst into flames while attempting to take off to attack the railway marshalling yards at Hildesheim, Germany.   Thankfully, the pilot (Flying Officer Horace Payne) and his crew were able to get well away before the bomb load, which included a 4,000lb 'cookie', detonated. [Photo. *Canada DND/PL44939*]

1945. This photograph taken c. 1945, shows the Ironmasters' District and the Newport area of Middlesbrough through the industrial haze that was the predominant feature of the town during those times, and which may have been one reason why intended targets were not always hit by the Luftwaffe's bombs.

The white areas, which stand out so clearly in the foreground, pinpoint those locations where bomb damage was so severe that the sites had to be cleared. The proximity of the sites to the railway line and the Ironmasters' District beyond would suggest the raiders had legitimate industrial targets in mind when they launched their attacks.

On 16 May, 1941, the lower gasometer provided a frighteningly spectacular display during an attack on the town. One of the six bombs dropped on that occasion exploded inside the gas tank and bomb fragments made '..*hundreds of holes..*' in the steel casing. The container continued to burn like a giant blow-torch until plucky Corporation workers were able to plug each hole—not a job to be envied!. [Photo. *Author's collection*]

County Borough of Middlesbrough

To WILLIAM NORMAN — C.D. Warden

This Certifies ~

that you have served your fellow citizens with unselfish credit and unassuming distinction, and have undertaken loyal service to our beloved country during our time of peril from enemy air raids in the European War, 1939 to 1945. By your achievements and sacrifice of time and convenience you have earned the gratitude of the people of Middlesbrough.

The Middlesbrough Civil Defence Committee hereby acknowledges on behalf of the whole community their profound gratitude, warm appreciation and their most grateful thanks.

Chairman of the Civil Defence Committee.

Town Clerk and A.R.P. Controller

A Certificate of Service was issued to all who had been members of the Civil Defence Forces during the war. This particular example was presented to the author's father, a World War One veteran who served in the ARP and the Home Guard during World War Two.

8th June, 1946

TO-DAY, AS WE CELEBRATE VICTORY, I send this personal message to you and all other boys and girls at school. For you have shared in the hardships and dangers of a total war and you have shared no less in the triumph of the Allied Nations.

I know you will always feel proud to belong to a country which was capable of such supreme effort; proud, too, of parents and elder brothers and sisters who by their courage, endurance and enterprise brought victory. May these qualities be yours as you grow up and join in the common effort to establish among the nations of the world unity and peace.

George R.I.

Schoolchildren received an acknowledgement of the fact that they too had 'shared the hardships and dangers of a total war'. This particular example was presented to the author—many years ago!.

STOCKTON HIPPODROME

9.0—NEXT WEEK—10.0.

Virginia Bruce ✦ Dennis Morgan
IN
FLIGHT ANGELS
with WAYNE MORRIS, RALPH BELLAMY, JANE WYMAN.
(Showing 3.25, 6.0, 5.35). ALSO SHOWING

TWO FOR DANGER
Featuring
BARRY K. BARNES ✦ GRETA GYNT

GOOD FRIDAY, 5.30 to 10.30.

THE AVENUE | MODERNE
NORTON-ON-TEES

Mon., Tues., Wed., 6.0 Cont. 10.10.
Anne Shirley and James Ellison in
ANNE OF WINDY WILLOWS (U)
Also showing LEON ERROL in
POP ALWAYS PAYS (U)
Thur. YOU WILL REMEMBER (U)

Mon., Tues., Wed., 6.0 Cont. 10.6.
WALTER BRENNAN and FAY
BAINTER in
MARYLAND (U)

Thur. FORTY LITTLE MOTHERS (U)

MAYFAIR CINEMA Lanehouse Rd., Thornaby
CONTINUOUS FROM 5.30.

Mon., Tues., Wed., April 7, 8, 9.
Hugh Herbert and Baby Sandy in
LITTLE ACCIDENT (U)
Also Days of Jesse James (U)

Thurs., Fri., Sat., April 10, 11, 12.
Richard Denning and Jean Cagney in
GOLDEN GLOVES (A)
Also Knights Of The Range (U)

CENTRAL, THORNABY. | QUEEN'S, THORNABY.

Mon., Tues., Wed., Cont. 5.45.
Ann Sheridan and Humphrey Bogart in
IT ALL CAME TRUE (A)
Thurs., Fri., Sat.: The Adventures of
Robin Hood (U)

Mon., Tues., Wed., Cont. from 5.45.
DR. CYCLOPS (A) (in Technicolor)
Starring Albert Dekker
Thurs., Fri., Sat.: Maryland (U)
(Technicolor)

EMPIRE MIDDLESBRO'
6-0—'Phone 2346—8-0
The North's Finest Variety Theatre. Week Commencing April 7, 1941

CAPERS AND SAUCE
Served by
ARTHUR WHITE THE FAMOUS LANCASHIRE COMEDIAN
Supported by
CICELY TREMAYNE ✦ JACK MARTYN
MUSICAL ELLIOTTS
KAROLLA DANCERS

PERFORMANCES AS USUAL, GOOD FRIDAY

Seats may be Reserved from 10 a.m. to 1.30 p.m. and 2.30 p.m. to 5 p.m.
6-0 P.M. YOU CAN GET A BUS HOME FROM THE EMPIRE 8-0 P.M.

6-0 THEATRE ROYAL 8-0
TWICE NIGHTLY. MIDDLESBROUGH. Tel. 3544.

COM. APRIL 7. SIXTH TERRIFIC WEEK. THE
ROYAL REPERTORY PLAYERS
PRESENT

Monday, Tuesday, Wednesday:
MARIA MARTIN
(or the Murder in the Old Barn)

Thursday, Friday, Saturday:
WHY GIRLS GO WRONG
(Or the Bonny Banks of Loch Lomond)

EMPIRE, WEST HARTLEPOOL

8 p.m.—TWICE NIGHTLY—8 p.m. Matinee To-day, Saturday, at 2.30.

TO-NIGHT, Last Two Performances of JACK TAYLOR'S LATEST PRODUCTION
EVE ON LEAVE
Including NAT MILLS and BOBBIE, GANJOU BROTHERS, and JUANITA, ERNEST
SHANNON, and MEXANO and his ACCORDION BAND.

Next Week: Special Attraction—RADIO FANFARE, including The Two Leslies, Suzette
Tarri, Billy Matchett, Joe Peterson, and Full Company.

REGENT | PALLADIUM

REGENT
MIDDLESBROUGH.

Monday, Tuesday, Wednesday,
SHOOTING HIGH (U)
TWO BIG PICTURES.
OH! JOHNNY HOW YOU CAN LOVE (U)

Thursday, Friday, Saturday.
Jeanette MacDONALD
NELSON EDDY in
NEW MOON (U)

PALLADIUM
MIDDLESBROUGH.
Continuous from 5.30.
Matinee: Mon., Wed., Fri., Sat., 2.15.
Mon., Tues., and Wed. Next.

NANCY KELLY
JON HALL in
SAILOR'S LADY (U)

Thur., Fri. and Sat. Next.
Jeanette MacDONALD
NELSON EDDY in
NEW MOON (U)

All Seats Bookable. 'Phone 3512.

REGENT · REDCAR

TO-MORROW (SUNDAY) at 7.30 p.m. Prices 2/3, 1/9, 1/3. NO BOOKING FEE.
Doors Open 7 p.m. Booking Office Open Sunday from 2 p.m.

OWEN WALTERS presents his FIFTH ANNIVERSARY
PROGRAMME Commencing his Sixth Year of Regent Concerts
with

ALFIE DUKES,
LESLIE FEENEY.

EDGAR DRIVER,
Popular B.B.C. Star Comedian.

IRIS BENTLEY,
Pianiste Supreme.

AUDREY CLEAVER,
Comedienne.

BOOTH HITCHIN, the Famous Covent Garden Baritone.

OWEN WALTERS and his BAND,
With Charlie Skinner, Judy Hutton, Rene Sherbourne.

April 7th.—Henry Wilcoxon, Carole Landis in MYSTERY SEA RAIDER
April 10th.—Anna Neagle, Ray Milland in IRENE

MARLBOROUGH, Middlesbro'
MATINEES DAILY AT 2.15 P.M.

Mon., Tues., Wed., April 7, 8, 9.
FREDERIC MARCH, JOAN BENNETT,
RALPH BELLAMY, ANN SOUTHERN,
ROBERT ELLIOTT in
TRADE WINDS (A)
And Full Supporting Programme.

Thurs., Fri., Sat., April 10, 11, 12.
LOUIS HAYWARD, TOM BROWN,
RICHARD CARLSON, JOAN FONTAINE,
ALAN CURTIS, KENNETH HARLAN in
THE DUKE OF WEST POINT (U)
And Full Supporting Programme.

ENTERTAINMENTS PAGE

ODEON THEATRES

ODEON, MIDDLESBROUGH

MONDAY, MAY 14th, 1945.　　SIX DAYS.

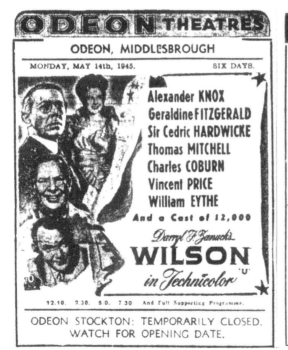

Alexander KNOX
Geraldine FITZGERALD
Sir Cedric HARDWICKE
Thomas MITCHELL
Charles COBURN
Vincent PRICE
William EYTHE
And a Cast of 12,000

Darryl F. Zanuck's

WILSON

in Technicolor "U"

12.10.　2.30.　5.0.　7.30.　And Full Supporting Programme.

**ODEON STOCKTON: TEMPORARILY CLOSED.
WATCH FOR OPENING DATE.**

REGENT - PALLADIUM

MIDDLESBROUGH.
Continuous from 2 p.m. Daily.

Monday, Tuesday, Wednesday:
TOM CONWAY :: MONA MARIS

The Falcon in Mexico
Showing at 3.25, 6.10, 8.55. (A)

RITA TERRY :: MARY LEE

Three Little Sisters
Showing at 2.0, 4.51, 7.36 (U)

Thursday, Friday, Saturday:
SPENCER TRACY, SIGNE HASSO

The Seventh Cross
Showing at 2.45, 5.31, 8.17. (A)
March of Time No. 5. Universal News, etc.

MIDDLESBROUGH.
Continuous 8.45.
Matinees Mon., Wed., Sat., 2.15.

Monday, Tuesday, Wednesday:
BASIL RATHBONE,
NIGEL BRUCE in

THE SCARLET CLAW

Thursday, Friday, Saturday:
JEANE CRAIN, JANE BALL in

WINGED VICTORY

REGENT - REDCAR

SUNDAY, MAY 13th.　Continuous from 6 p.m.

MARGARET LOCKWOOD,
MICHAEL WILDING in

DEAR OCTOPUS

Mon., Tues., Wed. Next:
The Musical Comedy,
ATLANTIC CITY.
Constance Moore, Brad Taylor,
Jerry Colonna, Paul Whiteman,
Louis Armstrong, at 2.55, 5.40, 8.25
Also PISTOL PACKIN' MAMA,
at 1.45, 4.30, 7.15.

Thursday, Friday, Saturday-Next:
Katharine Hepburn, Walter Huston,
Akim Tamiroff,

DRAGON SEED
At 3.5, 4.50, 7.35.
Note Times: Please Come Early!

Sunday,
May 13th:
Joseph Cotton.
Teresa Wright in

Cont from
6 p.m.

**CENTRAL
SHADOW OF DOUBT**

SCALA

Mon. Tues. Wed.　　Thurs Fri Sat
CONTINUOUS 1.30.　　FOR SIX DAYS.

THE MARX BROS.,
ALLAN JONES, KITTY CARLISLE in

A NIGHT AT THE OPERA
2.30, 5.10, 7.50. (U)

THE MEMPHIS BELLE
(Technicolor)

GAUMONT ⊕ HIPPODROME

MIDDLESBROUGH.　GAUMONT BRITISH THEATRES.

Continuous from 12.10.

Claudette COLBERT
Jennifer JONES
Joseph COTTON
Shirley TEMPLE
Monty WOOLLEY in

SINCE YOU WENT AWAY
At 12.30, 3.45, 6.55 (U)

HOW TO PLAY GOLF
(Colour Cartoon) U
At 12.10, 3.20, 6.40.

Continuous from 1.30 Daily.

MYSTERY! DRAMA! SUSPENSE!

LAURA
Starring (X)
GENE TIERNEY,
DANA ANDREWS.
Screening at 2.40, 5.25, 8.10.

Also a Really Thrilling Travelogue,

DANGEROUS JOURNEY
At 1.40, 4.20, 7.5. (A)

Come to the Matinee
Junior Club Every Saturday
at 9.30 a.m.

PAVILION

Mon. Tues. Wed.　　　Cont. from 4.40.

Paul Lukas, Carl Esmond in ADDRESS UNKNOWN (A) at 6.0, 8.35
Also June Clyde, Chick Chandler in SEVEN DOORS TO DEATH (A) at
4.50, 7.30.
To-day: HIGHER AND HIGHER.

105　　Cinema entertainment on Teesside for the week that the war ended.

Information regarding the 1939-45 period in the Teesside/Cleveland area is not easy to come by: written sources seem to be meagre in the extreme and most information appears to rest in the minds of those whose lives were touched by the events of the time. Thus my quest for personal recollections continues.

If there are readers of this volume who have experiences that they are willing to share—or photographs or memorabilia that they are willing to allow to be copied—I would be very interested to hear from them. No incident should be considered too small: it is the small detail that helps to make the total picture possible.

Bill Norman,
23a Thames Avenue,
Guisborough,
Cleveland, TS14 8AE

Printed by:
Thurston Printers
6 Amber Street, Saltburn-by-the-Sea, Cleveland TS12 1DT
Telephone: (01287) 623756
E-mail: ged@thurstonprinters.co.uk
www.thurstonprinters.co.uk